Creative

A Prayer

Devotional

Classic

E. Herman

First published in the United States by Harper and Brothers, this Forward Movement Miniature Book edition is slightly condensed from the original version by permission of the publisher.

Contents*

*The original edition contained another chapter on "The Priesthood of Prayer."

1

Prayer as Creative Energy

A radiant young girl, the daughter of a wealthy silk merchant of Lyons, was dancing at a fashionable ball. Her gown was the richest, her face the loveliest, and her step the lightest in all that gay assembly. She was engaged to the most popular young man in her social set, and the wedding was due within a week.

Suddenly, in the middle of a minuet, her foot faltered and her eyes grew wide and misty, as she looked past her partner into what had become to her a dull blur of colors. A vision had come to her, suddenly, unaccountably, wiping out the gay scene and fixing her eyes upon Eternity.

She, the careless butterfly of only a moment ago, had seen the vision of a dying world. In that flash of unearthly intuition she knew, with the unshakable certainty of the soul that has been touched by God, that the world was dying for lack of prayer. The world was perishing for lack of man's vital air. It was cut off from the very source of life, slowly dying the death of the asphyxiated. She seemed to hear its labored breathing—uneven, stertorous, spasmodic. She saw creation sink into nothingness and no one there to save, no one even to recognize the peril. Her friends were dancing around her, unaware that it was a dance of death. In a corner a smiling, debonair priest discussed the relative merits of eligible young men with a match-making mother. What chance had a dying world when the Church herself was drugged in slumber!

But God was watching, and had of His inscrutable mercy awakened her. Why? Why did she stand there, the only watcher among somnambulists? With a swift, resolute motion of soul, intense as leaping flame, she there and then renounced all that life had to offer her, and vowed herself to ceaseless prayer on behalf of a dying world.

Deaf to the entreaties of parents and lover, impregnable with the strength of those who have seen, she entered a convent, and became the pioneer of one of the great Contemplative Orders, whose influence has gone far beyond the bounds of the Roman Church, and from which the greatest of Christian mystics and reformers have always sprung.

I

The nun of Lyons does not stand alone in her testimony. Through all the centuries men and women have been awakened to see that the world—yes, and the Church also —was dying for lack of prayer. Always and everywhere apostles of prayer have arisen, calling upon a materialized Church to cease from the busyness of merely institutional activities and give herself to the true business of prayer. At every great crisis in the world's history multitudes have rediscovered the secret of prayer, and a tidal wave of petition and intercession has swept through Christendom. But again and again, once the crisis was past and the tension slackened, the voice of prayer became faint and inarticulate, and soon there was only a thin trickle where once the flood had been.

There is much curiosity about prayer, and particularly

about its psychology; much speculation as to its results, especially in cases of physical and mental disease. But there is no indication that the investigation of prayer has led to serious, sustained, concentrated practice.

Why is this so? No single answer can be given to the question: human nature is too complex a thing to admit of an explanation that covers all the facts. One thing that readily suggests itself is that many people who begin with a serious concern about prayer are soon switched off the main issue by reading a multitude of books on prayer, and deluded into imagining that they have grasped the reality of prayer because they have gained a facile acquaintance with the various theories and methods of prayer. Another consideration, grim but unfortunately true, is that for nine modern Christians who can be got to take an interest in institutional work or Church finance, scarcely one will respond to a challenge to prayer. To put it bluntly, for the average person of today, the term "spiritual" is equivalent to unpractical, if not illusory.

But there is one reason for the dearth of prayer of which we have taken all too little account. Throughout the Church there are sincere, earnest, thoughtful people, sensitive to the finest issues and honestly striving to serve God, who look upon much praying, and especially upon meetings for corporate prayer, with undisguised suspicion, as based upon a crude and childish conception of God, and as resolving themselves into little more than opportunities for emotional display.

For generations we have, to all practical intents and purposes, regarded prayer, in a deplorably mechanical way, as a process of importunate pleading and begging. I am not referring to our deliberate theories of prayer—the best mind of the Church in all ages has held a noble theory of prayer—but to our practice. As a matter of fact, we have proceeded as if prayer consisted in asking for various temporal and spiritual blessings with reiterative intensity, implying that, provided we asked earnestly enough and persistently enough, God would surely respond to our cry. Preaching has kept pace with our enlarging thought of God, but there has been comparatively little direct teaching on prayer in the light of that larger conception, and that little far too theoretical. As a consequence, prayer has become to hundreds of men and women who have outgrown the traditional conception of God either a mere pious sentiment or an outworn superstition.

We suffer, in fact, from arrested development in prayer. Prayer is one of those things we take for granted, very much after the manner of William Law's Mundanus:

Mundanus is a man of excellent parts and clear apprehension. He is well advanced in age and has made a great figure in business. Every part of trade and business that has fallen in his way has had some improvement from him, and he is always contriving to carry any method of doing anything well to its greatest height. . . . The only one thing which has not fallen under his improvement, nor received any benefit from his judicious mind, is his devotion. This is in just the same poor state as it was when he was only six years of age, and the old man prays now in that little form of words which his mother used to hear him repeat night and morning. . . . If Mundanus sees a book of devotion he passes it by as he would a spelling book, because he remembers that he learnt to pray at his mother's knee.

8

Mundanus still lives among us, and may be found by the score in every Christian congregation. In his secular affairs he often shows a marked, and not always quite pleasant, astuteness; in his commerce with God he is positively puerile—a child in everything except the childlike heart, without which we cannot enter the Kingdom of God. He cannot say with F. W. Faber,

> *Thou broadenest out with every year,*
> *Each breadth of life to meet,*

for his conception of God—if indeed an inherited convention can be called a conception—is scarcely adequate to the intelligence of a thoughtful schoolboy.

II

"Lord, teach us to pray," pleaded the disciples. And our Lord gave them a norm of prayer which has nourished the faith and life of the Church of all ages, produced a science of prayer which is still in its infancy, and given exhaustless treasures of thought to the noblest minds. We of today, however, tend to deny that prayer can be taught in any sense. We insist upon its lyrical spontaneity. It is "the soul's sincere desire, uttered or unexpressed"—as natural as the cry of the new-born babe or the groan of the dying. It is, indeed, of the essence of genius: who can produce genius by dint of hard work?

This is one of the fallacies peculiar to the religious mind. In all other realms of human thought or activity, genius, so far from being regarded as a dispensation from rigid discipline, is looked upon as the only sufficient justification for the highest form of training. And in the case of so vital an achievement as prayer the discipline must be correspondingly thorough. It is not by merely forming study circles, or reading books on prayer, that we shall enter into its mysteries and know its power, but by a discipline *co-extensive with life itself*. Prayer is, in the last resort, worth exactly as much—or as little—as the man behind it. If the man who prays has an obstinate, prejudiced, undisciplined mind, his prayer will suffer from the same defects. If his desires are limited, gross, and ill-guided, so will his prayer be.

This does not mean, of course, that we can afford to wait with beginning to pray until we have secured the ideal presuppositions (as well try and learn to swim on a table) but simply that we must bear in mind from first to last that prayer is the expression of a life. Prayer is not the whole of the spiritual life, or even, taken by itself, the most important factor in it. It depends upon ulterior processes. It rises out of a hinterland which determines its quality. While the faithful practice of prayer cannot fail to react upon the personality, we cannot achieve true personality simply by praying for certain virtues. It is here that the average adult fails to transcend the notions of childhood. We still have a vague but persistent idea that all we need is simply to pray to be "made good." We may clothe that idea in quite ambitious language, but in its essence it is the same that possessed us when we were little children at our mother's knee; and the same sense of disappointment still overtakes us when, in some quiet moment, we realize that, with all our praying to be made wise and patient and upright, we are not really any richer in these qualities than we were before. We are slow to learn that effective prayer involves a constant interaction between the quality of soul we bring to our prayers and the sincerity of our desire. To pray to be made wise is the merest superstition, unless we bring to our prayer the kind of soul that is capable of acquiring wisdom. We are responsible not only for our prayers, but for providing the background against which prayer can energize. It is not too much, indeed, to say that for every thought we give to prayer itself—excepting, of course, the actual practice of prayer, which is vital at every stage—we should give ten to the life behind the prayer.

When we consider the fundamental nature of prayer, the importance of this background becomes clearly apparent. We have come to regard prayer very largely as a process by which man is to avail himself of the spiritual forces of the universe. Given the firm conviction that we live in a spiritual universe, and a demand based upon this conviction, and prayer yields sure results. The prayer of faith, we say, is subject to definite, readily ascertainable laws, and once we pray in accordance with these laws, all things are possible to us, for we are "wired with God," yoked with the forces of Omnipotent Goodness. We can remove mountains of difficulty which before seemed insuperable, and call into being whole continents of good "out of nothing." And we argue that the sole reason why miracles do not follow prayer today is that the wave of materialistic science has left a stubborn sediment of fundamental unbelief in the triumph of spirit over matter.

But while this view represents one aspect of prayer, and that an aspect which modern psychology has made particularly attractive, it does not touch the heart of the subject. To know what prayer really is, we must study it from the center. And its central significance is not that of a spiritual process by which mountains are removed and benefits evoked. Prayer in its essence is communion with God. The simplest analogy—that of loving, trustful intercourse between friend and friend—is also the most profound.

The conception of prayer as the soul's secret, intimate converse with God is neglected by many, because it seems to them to make of prayer a narrowly individualistic exercise. But we do not argue after this fashion when the intimacies of the family or of friendship are concerned. We find it quite natural and reasonable that the life and influence of even the most altruistic of public men should be crucially determined by the sacred relationships of home. We are quite ready to admit the fact that a man's home life and friendships have more to do with his work for the world than a whole lifetime of public activity. It is a truism which we never dream of questioning. But we seem curiously reluctant nowadays to believe that the prayer of friendship with God is the most influential type of prayer. To realize that it is indeed so, one need only read the biographies of men whose lives have been nourished by prayer. Without a single exception, the type of prayer that shaped their lives and overflowed in blessing upon their generation was not so much a deliberate moral and spiritual process—the pressing of the button that releases creative energy, the scientific establishment of contact with the power-house of Divine electric force—but simple communion with their Heavenly Father. To them faith meant primarily not belief in the availability and efficiency of spiritual forces, and in the definiteness and uniformity of the laws which govern them, but personal trust, deepening from year to year with their deepening intimacy with God.

Once we grasp this, we shall realize that the condition of this prayer of communion is a right attitude of soul. As in human love and friendship, it is not moral perfection that is required. The most broken soul may enter that magic realm: who ever loved or was loved on account of mere moral excellence? Yet the soul that would know the secret of friendship must possess very definite moral and spiritual characteristics. It must be purged of prejudice and prepossession, and it must have a single eye towards the beloved. A man who approaches his friend chock-full of his own opinions and concerns, looking upon him only as affording welcome opportunity for self-expression, will never get beyond the outer court of the temple. Nor will one who is embarrassed with a thousand rival occupations and interests ever learn to spell the name of friend aright.

III

We are met, on the very threshold of prayer, by a moral demand. Friendship with God presupposes the beginnings of genuine humility and of fundamental simplicity of aim. Without humility—that is, without reality—there can be no power in prayer.

We all tend to be infatuated with the idea of strength—that is why definitions of prayer in terms of force appeal to us strongly—but we fail to realize that all true strength is grounded in humility. We still relegate humility to the pale ranks of passive virtues and ornamental graces, whereas, in its legitimate development, it is a stout and soldierly quality. Humility, indeed, is simply a sense of reality and proportion. It is grounded upon a knowledge of the truth about ourselves and about God. "The reason why God is so great a Lover of humility," says St. Vincent de Paul, with his characteristic forthrightness, "is because He is the great Lover of truth. Now humility is nothing but truth, whilst pride is nothing but lying."

Humility stands for perfect sanity. It represents the life that is ranged round its rational center. It means that the soul has found its level in the world of reality. Every man who finds his center in self is on the way to madness—is, indeed, already a little mad.

At least one-half of what we miscall humility, especially the habit of self-accusation and self-abasement which passes for a deep sense of sin, is the fruit of self-obsession. The chronic depression and despondency which go along with a certain type of religious temperament are simply the outcome of lacerated pride. We are disappointed with ourselves, not because we are humble, but, quite on the contrary, because we thought too highly of ourselves, and are wounded in our pride. Pride is known most surely not by its swagger, but by its quickness to grow bitter and despondent. The soul that is truly humble takes its faults quietly, and goes on afresh in confidence and hope. For humility rests not upon self-contemplation, but upon a vision of God.

To approach God in prayer with humility is "to know what it means to be a created being, and to have a Creator." That seems the most elementary of truisms, but it includes the whole philosophy of prayer. To come to God as the Fountain of our being, the Inspirer of our prayers, the great Sustainer without whose upholding arm we must sink back into nothingness—how far removed such an attitude is from that in which we habitually draw near to Him! Our prayers are blighted by self-consciousness. When we are not

14

paralyzed by doubt, we are preoccupied with the recital of our woes and wrongs, our aspirations and ambitions. We tend to forget that in God we live and move and have our being, and to approach Him as if we had come to reason and plead with one like unto ourselves, "only bigger."

But is there not something akin to this humble sense of dependence in the highest human friendship? Is not love a sacrament that must be taken kneeling? We come to the friend of our heart, and as we open our soul to him we realize that it is of his own that we are giving him. That impulse of love, that worthy aspiration, that new outlook upon life—it is of his creating. As we are initiated into the mystery of friendship, we know that our friend is not merely "another"; he speaks to us not from without, but from the center of our being. He is in us and we in him. His influence is profoundly mystical; no merely temperamental affinity can account for friendship at its highest potency. Deep down in the abysmal mystery of being was the thread spun that linked soul to soul. My friend creates me and recreates me. In him I come to know my true self. His love and trust purge me of sin by shame and contrition; his gentleness makes me great; his high expectations make all things possible to me. And what is true in a limited measure of human friendship is wholly true of man's communion with his Creator, for the very act of creation is nothing else than the outgoing of Infinite Love. God loved us into being, and in acknowledging Him as our Maker we open our inmost nature to the Friend whose love is creative power and whose might is self-emptying love. Ever since we were born His creative and sustaining influence was upon us, and in the prayer of humility we consciously open our hearts to the Power that worked there from our earliest days without our conscious concurrence. We welcome the Love that has access to the most secret springs of our being, and lay our secrets bare to the Sympathy that knows us and we can never know ourselves. Knowing God as "the master-light of all our seeing," we know ourselves blind. Glimpsing the beauty of His holiness, we see ourselves stained and polluted. Hearing the voice of self-giving Love, the shame and misery of our soul cry out for redemption. Bowing in awe and penitence before the Almighty Judge, we know the secret of supreme friendship. Such is the great paradox of Christian prayer.

And the heart that desires the supreme friendship must be undivided in its aim. The grace of prayer is the grace of the single eye. When we read the lives of the saints, we are struck by a certain large leisure which went hand in hand with a remarkable effectiveness. They were never hurried; they did comparatively few things, and these not necessarily striking or important; and they troubled very little about their influence. Yet they always seemed to hit the mark; every bit of their life *told*; their simplest actions had a distinction, an exquisiteness which suggested the artist. The reason is not far to seek. Their sainthood lay in their habit of referring the smallest actions to God. They lived in God; they acted from a pure motive of love towards God. They were as free from self-regard as from slavery to the good opinion of others. God saw and God rewarded: what else needed they? They possessed God and possessed themselves in God. Hence the inalienable dignity of these meek, quiet figures that seem to produce such marvellous effects with such humble materials.

But we of today scarcely ever possess ourselves. Our hearts are ceaselessly vexed with a mixed multitude of imaginings and aims. We belong to the movements and causes we are interested in, whereas it is they that should belong to us, if we were indeed Christ's, as Christ is God's. We no longer wait upon God at every turn; we are too hurried and distracted for such waiting. Our self-imposed duties tread on each other's heels, and when at last we compose ourselves for our final rest, we are conscious that, with all our doing, we have accomplished very little. For we lack that guarded heart, that grace of priestly discretion, which says, "I hold myself for God; I hold all other things in and for the sake of God."

To say God, and mean the world; to name Christ, and intend self—what state could be more deplorable? And so long as we come to prayer distracted by a multitude of interests which we have never yet brought to light of God's countenance, embarrassed by a thousand and one occupations concerning which we have never yet inquired the will of God, we shall still be seeking ourselves, no matter how urgently we address God. Friendship implies a heart at leisure from itself. The supreme friendship demands a singleness of devotion, a simplicity and perfection of "intention towards God," which spells liberty and power. It is purity of intention we need—the direction of our whole nature towards God. Where that intention is not only right but pure, steadfast, and consistently loving, God's creative energy flows into the spirit. The whole life is reordered after a Divine pattern, and henceforth bears the seal of a supernatural distinction. We know how an absorbing devotion to a great ideal or, more potently still, to a beloved person simplifies and unifies life. And to the soul that is wholly bent upon God, a thousand fretting cares and vexing problems which tear the lives of others in pieces simply cease to exist. With the submerging of the irrelevant, the soul is free to give itself to that which really matters. Life becomes thenceforth triumphantly effective. It is no more the happy hunting-ground of vagrant impulses and futile efforts; it is the theater of Divine activity, the sphere of creative power. Its circumference is governed from the center.

IV

It does not matter how we approach the subject, provided we come to real grips with it. Sooner or later we shall see that the many questions and difficulties which gather round the prayer life may be reduced to the one momentous question of our relationship to Him with whom we desire to hold communion. What about our relation to God? That is the question which we are inclined to shirk, but which mercifully refuses to be silenced. It persists through all philosophical evasions and theological hairsplitting, through all intellectual doubts and moral problems. There are many valid difficulties about prayer, and we must face them; but in grappling with them we shall come to see that they are not fundamental, and that their solution depends upon our attitude to a deeper problem.

Let us put it quite plainly. The real question at issue is whether we have the kind of relation to God that is the only basis of prayer at its highest and best. We are not dealing here with the universal human need of prayer. No one can doubt for a moment that the cry wrung from a soul in bitter need and anguish—the prayer of parents for their dying children, the pleading of those that gather round sickbeds, the inarticulate ejaculation of a soul suddenly face to face with its sin—is genuine prayer and swiftly reaches the heart of God. What we are concerned with is Christian prayer in its full potency—the prayer of faith that removes mountains, that high commerce with God which is concentrated creative energy.

As we consider prayer at the level at which it becomes a channel of creative power, most of the difficulties which surround its more elementary aspects will be resolved. For prayer, like any other human activity, can only be judged rightly by observing its normal manifestations; and it is not the more common, but the rarer forms of prayer, which represent the normal. The lower forms—the spasmodic instinctive cry of need—are instances of arrested development, and it is as unfair to measure prayer by them as to judge the strength of the human body from observing an invalid. Not the frenzied cry of sudden anguish, but the calm, trustful committal of faith, is the normal attitude of the praying soul. Not the answered prayer of the mother whose child is spared, but the apparently unanswered prayer of our Lord in the Garden, is the classic instance.

We see that prayer, so far from being a tiresomely reiterated asking, based upon a conception of God that belongs to the childhood of the race, is the highest and most dynamic form of interaction between the human and the Divine. It is the whole personality—intellect as well as emotion and will—energizing in fellowship with the Lord of all Life. It is man consciously apprehending his high destiny and stretching towards it. It is not merely one of the noblest and most fruitful activities of the soul, at once the most intensely individual and the most comprehensively social, but the fount and the consummation of all noble activity.

The fatal habit of contrasting prayer and action is deeply ingrained in the modern mind, and we persist in taking it as a mere figure of speech when we hear prayer defined as a succession of vital acts. The old prejudice against what is called the contemplative state survives, and sustained prayer continues to be regarded by the majority of sensible people as suitable only for invalids and others who are debarred from an active life.

But the moment we make an honest attempt to get at the central meaning of beneficent activity, we find that its fundamental significance is identical with that of prayer. What, after all, is the most important function of the active worker, say, in the slums of some large city? It is not to relieve poverty merely, or to lessen the sum of human misery. Indeed, it might be argued that in protracting the lives of the feeble, the diseased, and the generally inefficient, such a worker actually adds to the sum of human misery in helping to perpetuate a defective type. But the central object and the most potent effect to the worker's activity is, in reality, something quite different. It is positive, not negative. It consists not in alleviating suffering, but in creating an atmosphere in which faith and hope, selfless love and devoted service, health and happiness become not only possible but easy and natural. His pity purges the fetid spiritual atmosphere; his devotion propagates itself and kills the noisome growths of selfishness, as the germs of health overcome the bacilli of disease; his consecrated personality releases imprisoned powers of good in the most unlikely quarters. As he goes about his work, he restores the choked wells of trust and healing in the embittered of the poor, and liberates the tide of brotherhood in the sealed hearts of the rich. He awakens high aspirations in the denizens of mean streets, and inspires heroic devotion in the children of privilege. Any material amelioration or social reform which he may secure is a by-product of this central process; its excellence depends entirely upon its connection with it. War has revealed to us the essential sordidness and hopelessness of social progress which does not spring from a heart of religious devotion. We have seen how the brute in man thrives under advanced economic, social, and intellectual conditions. It would almost seem that whereever social reform is based upon no sanctions beyond itself; there it becomes the breeding ground of a new race of human apes and tigers, more shapely on the surface but more monstrous within than the old beasts of the slum jungle.

Argue as we may, the saints were right. The central source of all genuinely beneficent activity is prayer. The man who "merely" prays, if it be the prayer of communion with God, is more truly a benefactor of the race than he who endows a children's home; and the time will come when the great philanthropies will be traced back to their source in the prayers of humble, obscure folk whom the world agreed to despise. Nothing good can ever come to man except by man's union with the creative energy of God—a union which is unconsciously present in germ wherever a soul is on fire with love and compassion, and consciously realized in the prayer of communion.

Such prayer—prayer which changes both the man who prays and the world he lives in—is not achieved without concentrated effort. It demands a committal of soul, a self-surrender, which takes us into the deepest heart of religion. To make this surrender is to become a high priest of Divine mysteries. But while there are those who in a flash, as it were, pass from the market place to the Holy of Holies, most souls need to traverse the outer court and to tarry in the place of preparation. Two trusty aids await us there: Silence and Meditation. They are not mysterious and fanciful pursuits, peculiar to the high-strung devotees of mystical cults. They are, on the contrary, part of the natural discipline of the healthy soul bent upon communion with God. They are as simple as daylight, and as sensible as reason itself.

2

The Ministry of Silence

We have been accustomed to regard the cultivation of
silence as part of an esoteric mechanism, or, if we believe
it to be a genuine spiritual discipline, as exclusively connected with contemplative prayer. We look upon it as a
counsel of perfection for persons of large leisure and of
meditative turn of mind, who aspire to those high grades
of prayer which seem to us dangerously akin to trance
experiences and other psychic phenomena. What we need
to learn is that the practice of silence is sound wisdom for
common folk bent upon the prayer of intimate communion;
that, indeed, it is the preliminary discipline *par excellence*
for all who wish to enter the great world of prayer. The
sense of unreality which so insistently haunts the beginner
in prayer is due to the fact that he is engaged in a monologue and not in a conversion. For the object of prayer is
not merely to find expression for one's deepest yearnings,
but to converse with Another, to hear the Divine call, and
to feel the Divine response to the movement of the soul.
And it is as impossible to realize our communion with God
without the practice of silence, as it is to conduct a conversation *à seul* (by oneself).

As we approach prayer by the spacious antechamber of
silence, we come to realize that the first mover is not we,
but God. The prayer that rises to our lips as passionate

beseeching of a Father's care and sympathy is not an initial pleading: it is rather the response to an advance. Its very passion is inspired by the Spirit who broods over the soul's formless waters and brings articulate expression out of a voiceless waste of need. Prayer always begins with God. As the little child learns its first prayers from its mother's lips, the soul learns to pray from God. There is not a half formed aspiration or a heavenward impulse that was not first "inspoken" into the heart by the Spirit who maketh intercession for us. But we so often refuse to come to prayer through the antechamber of silence. We will not wait and listen for the prayers He is waiting to pray in and through us. And the result is a long, weary, discouraging monologue, which grows intolerable as we become aware of our aloneness. None except the vividly imaginative, who delight in weaving romances around themselves, can sustain the monologue indefinitely; after a time, the heart grows sick with hope deferred, and we abandon prayer as a dreary form of self-soliloquy—like a make-believe of talking through a telephone with no one listening at the other end.

Yet, did we but know it, a recourse to attentive silence would make even these self-willed prayers alive with the reality of the Divine response. The Spirit whom we disregarded in the framing of our prayers is waiting to guide them still, clarifying our vision, deepening our insight, taking of the hidden treasure of Christ and showing it to our [newly opened] eyes. When prayer seems a hallucination, the simple expedient of hushing the soul to silence often serves to assure us, past all doubting, of the reality of our contact with the Unseen. It is upon our willingness to listen and hear God speak that our prayer life from first to last depends. This should be clear when we remember that prayer is the soul's pilgrimage from self to God; and the most effectual remedy for self-love and self-absorption is the habit of humble listening.

I

Thoughtful men everywhere are awake to the therapeutic and recreative force of silence. It is the wisdom of the wanderer who, wearied and sore at heart, comes home at dusk, and is stabbed by his sense of strangeness amid the familiar surroundings of his own country.

We of today have lost the sure-footed certainty which our spiritual fathers had. We do not claim to have attained; we cannot even be said to press towards the mark, for the mark is often hidden from our dull and wavering eyes. But even though the goal looms dim in the mist and we are not quite certain of the way, we stand wistfully waiting for someone or something to set us on the path.

We wait, but lack the wisdom of them that wait. We wait impatiently, feverishly turning the pages of a hundred guidebooks, making voluble inquiries of this expert and that, embarking upon any and every adventure that tempts our vagrant fancy. We are even violent at times, but with all our violence we do not take the Kingdom by force.

Then, exhausted with our profitless gropings and flutterings, we listen, perchance, to a stray prophet who reminds us that there is such a thing as a divine science of waiting, and that its master key is silence—the deep, full stillness of the expectant soul. "Be still, and know that I am God."*

But we hesitate. The vogue of pseudomysticism, with its jargon about recollection, concentration, and "going into

* *Psalm* 46:10

the silence," has prejudiced us against the deliberate cultivation of spiritual stillness. And we also hesitate for another and deeper reason. We know that silence is indeed an unexplored realm, peopled with disquieting apparitions and brimful of unguessed terrors for the chance traveller. No one who has honestly tried to still his soul—to wean intellect and will and emotion from their external activity to a concurrent attitude of quiet expectancy—but has sensed possibilities of weird experiences compared to which the most "successful" spiritualistic séance would appear trite and tame.

For we too have sojourned too long in the dusty city of external relationships. We have gazed so fixedly and persistently upon the pageantry of passing things that they have become our only reality. We have lived so deeply in the lives of our neighbors and our community—and in the mere shell of their lives at that—that we have lost track of that mysterious "buried life" of ours which is the only real life we possess. Our very religion has become little more than a vigorous effort to be sociable and communicative. Impulses which should breed resolution in our souls are exhausted in resolutions on paper, and thoughts that should condense to strong purpose evaporate in a moist vapor of small talk. And, as a result, silence of any kind has become difficult. The moment the noise about us stops, we become disquieted and ill at ease. Accustomed to commune with anyone and everyone, we have lost the art of communing with our own spirits, and the prospect of such self-communing does not inspire us with confidence.

And yet a deep instinctive wisdom—part of our inheritance from an age when men dwelt alone and walked with God—tells us that in quietness lies our salvation. It has been well said that in the darkness the eyes are opened, and in silence the heart speaks. He, too, was a wise man who first discovered that in order to live we must stand aloof from what the crowd calls living; and so was that other unknown scribe who told us that "silent men are kings, for they rule over a great country where none can follow them." And if the stillness of self-communing is a veritable well of life and healing, what of that "silence of the soul that waits for more than man to teach?" Yes, we know ourselves to have been in the far country, and, having returned to our own land, our only wisdom is to close our eyes and wait humbly, "as one waits in the antechamber of the mighty," for the reconciling touch of God.

For, say what we will—and the conviction will not be accepted unchallenged by the mind of today—a discipline of solitude and silence is essential for those who would acquaint themselves with God and be at peace. We are living in an age which has discovered the meaning and value of corporateness. Fellowship is its watchword, and community of experience its aim. And the eye of the age has seen truly, for until the individual knows himself as a member of corporate humanity, his personal experience must remain fragmentary and barren. We are in sober truth members one of another, and it is only in fellowship that we can realize God's purpose.

But where we are continually led astray is in confounding vital corporateness either with mere gregariousness, or with sociability and communicativeness, or with outward uniformity of opinion and action. All these may exist apart from any vital fellowship. They are, in fact, not essential to fellowship at all, and often constitute its most stubborn hindrance. The solitary worshipper who really touches God, and touches Him not with a merely self-regarding motive, but with a heart of love for all men and a tender fellow feeling with human need and woe, is engaged in a more genuine act of fellowship than a thousand gregarious individuals who mistake external togetherness for vital unity. Such a man is worshipping with the whole Church Catholic,* and, like his Lord, seeks to sanctify himself for his brethren's sake. We need not decry togetherness; it is a necessity for the normal human being, and experiences are possible to a company of men of one heart and mind which are not possible for even the noblest and saintliest individual alone. But we constantly tend to take it for granted that mere togetherness is equivalent to true unity, and that the man who feels within himself the Divine call to solitude and silence is thereby cutting himself off from the fellowship. Such an assumption is entirely contrary to fact.

It is not without significance that the earliest spirituality of the post-Apostolic Church ran along the line of solitude and silence. We are repelled, if not positively appalled, by the picture of the Fathers of the Desert limned with such scrupulous fidelity by Palladius in his book *Paradise*. Their ruthless violence to every natural instinct; their severe, and often grotesque and even disgusting, physical austerities; their narrow outlook and stern piety; all combine to make them particularly unattractive to an age which counts all natural impulses divine. And yet no impartial reader of these strange lives and collections of remarkable sayings can avoid the conclusion that, however deplorable their eccentricities and excesses, these men were profoundly right in believing that he who wants to be the friend of Christ must forsake much that the world counts friendship; that

* *Universal*

28

he who desires to see God must close his eyes to many things which the world thinks desirable; and that he who wishes to hear the voice of the Spirit must stop his ears against the babel of tongues and put a seal upon his lips. Their lives bore irrefutable witness to the truth that was in them. The wisdom that is foolishness with men was never justified more convincingly than in these children of the desert.

For as we read their histories, we realize that there, in the silence of the wilderness, amid the grim exactions of a merciless ideal, the very humanities in whose name we protest against such an ideal came to birth and were fostered. Did a sick or friendless stranger need food, lodging, and careful nursing? It was in the rocky cells of the wilderness he got it. For to the Fathers of the Desert hospitality was a duty that ranked higher than almost any other, and when a stranger came to a hermit's door, the holy man would ply him with the best of food at his command, and, in the true spirit of delicate hospitality, break his fast and eat with him. Did a heartbroken sinner, scorned by the world and cast out by the Church seek compassion and tender human sympathy? It was to the solitaries that he turned in his bitter hour, for these austere and silent men had discovered the secret of Christ's love for the outcast, in an age when the Church had already forgotten it. Did famine or pestilence scourage the cities? It was to the men of the desert they sent to tend the sick, organize collections, and superintend the distribution of food. It was these men, whom we like to regard as inhuman and unpractical that tried to alleviate the misery of prisoners thirteen centuries before Elizabeth Fry, sent camel and boat loads of food to the half-starved populations of remote cities, and, in an age when tenderness to animals was looked upon as an unpleasant kind of madness, anticipated St. Francis in their idyllic relations to the wild beasts and their kindliness towards every living thing.

Robert Louis Stevenson, in his spirited defense of Father Damien [the leper's friend], met the jibes of the priest's critics, who accused him of uncleanly habits, by reminding them that it was this man of doubtful cleanliness who had provided a clean abode for those whom the rest of the world had left in filth and misery. "There was not a pan or a pot on Molokai that dirty Damien had not washed." And so it might be said of the Fathers of the Desert that there was not a kindly and humane impulse within the Christendom of that day that did not find its pioneer and apostle among the gaunt "inhuman" ascetics of the wilderness. They turned their backs upon a world that thought them mad, and proved their sublime sanity by the fruits they brought from the land of silence and poverty. Charities beside which our modern institutions seem dismal and lifeless; a sense of spiritual values to which we are only now approximating very slowly; a brotherliness towards all feeble, needy, broken things, and especially towards erring womanhood, which the Church of today has still to learn —these and many other gifts they bequeathed to the ages to come.

And it has ever been thus. The great silent men, who judged even lawful pleasures inexpedient for Christ's athletes, and voluntarily narrowed their lives and emptied themselves of many things they would jealously have coveted had they not coveted the One Thing even more jealously—it has always been they who anticipated the world's greatest reforms, inspired it with its noblest ideals, brought loveliness out of the unlovely, and by their poverty made many rich. They were not all ascetics in the conventional sense, but they were all lovers of silence, and not afraid to dwell apart. Doing their work in the world, they made time for quiet brooding, for large and heroic solitude, even though that time had to be stolen from social joys, or wrested from sleep.

If we read the biographies of the great and wise, be they statesmen or priests, teachers or poets, Roman Catholics or Quakers, we shall find that they were men of long silences and deep ponderings. Whatever of vision, of power, of genius there was in their work was wrought in silence. And when we turn to the inner circle of the spiritual masters—the men and women, not necessarily gifted or distinguished, to whom God was "a living, bright reality" which supernaturalized their everyday life and transmuted their homeliest actions into sublime worship—we find that their roots struck deep into the soil of spiritual silence. Living in the world and rejoicing in human relationships, they yet kept a little cell in their hearts whither they might run to be alone with God.

II

We know that this is so. We too have tried to practice this pregnant silence, but the results have been disappointing. When we tried to hush our souls in solitude, we have found it a difficult and futile experiment. To begin with, we were torn asunder by a thousand and one distractions. Scarcely had we resolved to be silent, when a swarm of intruding thoughts, many of them absurdly irrelevant, laid seige to our souls. Trifles that had not caused us a moment's reflection before, suddenly assumed a morbid importance.

Considerations we would have brushed aside under any other circumstances, presented themselves again and again with grotesque insistence and we were helpless against them. Business problems and family cares pressed upon us with a weight they never had previously. Then we became acutely conscious of our bodies, which rebelled against the unwonted stillness. Every nerve grew superacutely sensitive. The ticking of the clock, the crackling of a log in the grate, the slightest sound or movement became a small torture to the sensitive, and tried the temper of the more robust.

And when at last we gained the upper hand of these distractions, one of two things happened. Either our silence degenerated into idle daydreaming, or the enervating mist of undifferentiated feeling, or merely a dull emptiness that left one yawning. Or else it sharpened into a state of a futile expectancy. It became dense, strained, uncanny. The tension was that of painful listening, as of one who strains his ear for the sound of a football which he knows in his heart will never come. And it all ended in a loss of vitality. One's tone was lowered. After all this expenditure of vital force, one was left with nothing more substantial than the weakness of reaction from a purely artificial strain. It was as if a man had clenched his fist and driven it, with all the weight of his muscle, into the empty air.

We have looked for the cause of our failure to achieve the dynamic silence of the saints in every direction but the right one. The brooding silence of the saints in which so many great things were born seems incompatible with a twentieth century background. They lived in days of spiritual leisure, when problems were few and simple, and a dormant social conscience allowed them to concentrate upon the business of "making their souls." In our day things are different.

But the truth lies elsewhere. The one fact we forget is that the saints were capable of spiritual silence simply because they had not contracted our modern habit of ceaseless talk in their ordinary life. Their days were days of silence, relieved by periods of conversation, while ours are a wilderness of talk with a rare oasis of silence.

It is useless to imagine that one can pass at a bound from a daily round in which the lust of talk absorbs three-fourths of the soul's energy to a state of harmonious, revealing stillness. The practice of silence must begin, not in the office and the home, the playing field and the Church. The soul whose virility has been allowed to ooze out through the tongue during eleven hours of the day, need not hope to regain it during the silent twelfth hour. To put it bluntly, the first step towards attaining interior quiet is to hold one's peace more frequently and to better purpose in the ordinary ways of life. "Silence," says Thomas Carlyle, "is the element in which great things fashion themselves together, that at length they may emerge full formed and majestic into the daylight of life which they are henceforth to rule. Do thou thyself but hold thy tongue for one day, and on the morrow how much clearer are thy purpose and duties; what wreck and rubbish have the mute workmen within thee swept away when intrusive noises were shut out!"

We have yet to accept and act upon the axiom that the cultivation of a habit of silence is an integral part of all true education; and that children, so far from looking upon a demand for silence as an unnatural and intolerable imposition, have an inborn aptitude for quietness.

This insistence upon man's need for silence, quite apart from any definitely religious motive or object, seems elementary and pedestrain, but it needs reiterative emphasis in this age of loud disputes and weak convictions. The other day I chanced to talk to a strong, plain working woman whose mastery over adverse circumstances was little short of heroic. She had much to say concerning the simple habit of silence. "When I was a little girl," she remarked, "my mother taught me that arnica was good for bruised flesh, and silence was good for a bruised soul; and she made me apply both whenever they were needed." The soul that knows how to be silent in the ordinary vicissitudes of life is the soul that will most readily master the art of spiritual quiet and recollection.

So, after all, the queer fake culture of silence, with its jargon about concentration and "coming into tune with the Infinite," and its cheap paraphernalia of crystals and magic mirrors and breathing exercises, is based upon the recognition of a real need, to which many of those who sneer at it are pathetically blind. The Church especially has still to learn what many a poor "crank" has learned long ago— that we frail, distracted children of men have no chance of hearing the voice of God until we have learned to be silent and listen. The spiritual realities do not shriek and shout, and it still remains true that Jesus comes "the doors being shut." It was high wisdom, if poor exegesis, that made the mystical instinct interpret those shut doors as the resolute quieting of the soul which is necessary before the Christ can enter. When the saints and mystics desired the Vision of visions, they first shut the soul's doors, "for fear of the Jews." It is not Christian liberty, but sheer dullness of spirit, that frees us from a wholesome fear of that "mixed multitude" of thoughts, concerns, and motives that turns the soul's sanctuary into a marketplace where the voice of Jesus is drowned in the clamor of jangling impulses. Before we have any real right even to discuss the difficulties of communion with God we must have resolved, at the cost of whatever hardship to our relaxed and dissipated souls, to learn the secret of silence.

III

More especially we must learn to cultivate a deep reticence regarding the affairs of the soul. Who that has searched the deeps of his heart can doubt the truths of this? Our prayers are thin and perfunctory in exact proportion as our tongues are glib and gratuitously communicative. By the time we have talked a subject threadbare, we have evaporated its essence, and when at last we think of setting it before God, we are overtaken by a humiliating sense of emptiness and futility. The thing that had swelled to such gratifying dimensions under the genial influence of discussion, is, in the light of the Eternal, seen to be a mere mote of small dust. As a matter of fact, we feel disinclined to pray about it at all, at least in private; and this is a healthy sign, for it means that there is at least one corner of our life in which we cannot tolerate a sham. It probably began as a reality, but we have talked it into a sham. It is no longer part of us. It is something quite external to our true selves—an occupation, not a vocation.

And if we trace this dismal business to its root, we shall find that what our habit of talking has done for us is really to undermine the very foundations of our spiritual life. If prayer has any reality at all, it is founded upon a sense of God, and as it develops into something more than an occasional spasmodic cry under the pressure of need or anguish, our sense of God becomes a dominant factor in our lives. We are learning the habit of referring everything to Him, and measuring everything by His standard.

We are slow to realize that the so-called religious world is still—the world. Those who are inside that "religious" world are duped by it, and those who are outside are tragically prejudiced against religion itself by identifying it with that conventional religiosity whose hollowness they are quick to discern. The Christian who lives in slavish deference to the religious world is, in effect, a living negation of the very soul of Christianity. It all runs back to this in the end: whether we mean to live in the light of God, or in the light of the world; and if we choose the latter, prayer becomes not only difficult, but, in its full sense, impossible.

What old spiritual writers used to call "human respect" —that enslavement to the opinion of our fellows which is responsible for nine-tenths of the futility of our lives— lies at the root, not only of our inability, but also of our more or less pronounced disinclination for solitary communion with God. Under its domination the world is always with us. We may enter into our closet and shut the door, that we may pray to our Father who seeth in secret; but scarcely have we turned the key in the lock, when the omnipresent company invades our solitude, blotting out the Divine Presence and filling the silence with a myriad distracting tongues. We are beset by an inquisitorial world specter. It is as though the gaze of all mankind had been focused in one piercing, inescapable eye, and concentrated upon our soul. To live beneath that intimidating glare is a slavery so galling that, as one has well said, the austerities of a Carthusian monastery might be easier to bear. It turns religion into an irksome imposition, if not into a positive torment, and makes of life a tawdry stage play—a hollow, heartless, spectacular affair, in which convention takes the place of right, prudential wisdom supplants character, and public opinion usurps the Judgment seat of God.

This "human respect," which is innate in every soul but gets its chance through the habit of ceaseless talk, and grows with the growth of our loquacity concerning things that are meant to be wrapped in silence, is at once the most puerile and the most noxious of our many present day superstitions.

In the end this love of talk, which at the worst we regard as an amiable weakness, breeds that cowardly and servile temper which is the antipodes of dynamic prayer. For if prayer be indeed a great adventure, a giving of all for all, a staking of a man's whole life upon an unseen good whose only pledge is the Cross, then only the brave can pray. The essential servility of the talkative is, as a rule, concealed from us, because such persons have a very ambitious conception of what is due to them, and insist somewhat violently upon their rights. But, in reality, the soul that empties itself of its most intimate treasure in talk delivers itself over into a state of helplessness and slavery. Its clamorous self-assertiveness is the measure of its servile dependence upon the esteem and approval of its circle. Such a soul will never attain to vital communion with God. It may, indeed, have a remarkable facility in prayer—souls of this type are often temperamentally inclined to expansive devotions—but it will always stop short of the kind of prayer that transmutes life into power and victory.

Everyone who knows anything about the interior life knows that there is indeed a moment in our communion with God in which the soul knows itself to be alone with Him in the world, and knows also that in that august aloneness lies peace and power. It was in His hours of solitary communion with the Father, when all other presences receded before the one overshadowing, all-inclusive Presence, that Jesus heard the cry of the world's life and looked deep into its heart. It was then that He divined the uttermost of human need and sorrow. "Close to the heart of the Eternal Father, He learned to love men, to see their misery, to understand God's purpose for them, to perceive the true meaning of sin. He leaves the world, and His reward is to know human life as none other ever knew it, to suffer, to pray, and to die for it."

"It is no small matter," says Thomas à Kempis, "to keep silence in an evil time." Sorrow may be among God's mightiest angels, but it does not necessarily, and in itself, do angel's work. A time of sorrow is often a time of moral and spiritual relaxation, of weakening self-pity, and of incontinent demands upon the sympathy of others. It breeds self-importance rather than heroism. And the selfishness of sorrow feeds upon speech. Small wonder that the masters of the spiritual life have always held up as the ideal what old writers used to call "the virginity of suffering"—the habit of keeping silence concerning our sorrows to all except God! There is, of course, a limit to this counsel. Human sympathy of the right kind is sacramental, and God comforts His servants, as He comforted St. Paul, "by the coming of Titus." But while past ages tended to deny the Divine nature of human sympathy and fellowship, our own tends to idolize them. We again and again weaken ourselves, and others, and miss the Divine consolation, by running to this person and to that before we make our need known unto God. In the joy of our discovery of the sacredness of human affection, we forget that it remains unshakably true that whatever be the power of human sympathy, the soul of man is created for direct, immediate communion with its God. Nothing, however lovely and true in its own order, can take the place of that immediate touch. And that touch will not be experienced by a soul that has exposed itself to every well-meaning hand, in its feverish search for comfort.

Did we but know the things that belong to our peace in times of sorrow and adversity, our instinct of spiritual self-preservation would urge us to hug silence to our bosoms and to reserve our deepest confidences for God. And of all sorrows, those of the inward life most urgently call for silence. The vice of airing one's soul to any and every man whom we believe likely to prove sympathetic and helpful is eating the very core of reality out of those who practice it. There are times in our spiritual life when we need a human counselor and guide, but nowhere are wisdom and self-restraint more imperative than here. Our Protestant practice allows us to give free rein to our craving for sympathy, to pour out our confidences with as much profusion and intimacy of detail as we feel inclined to, and to go back upon the matter of our self-revelation as often as we choose, re-opening the same question again and again and keeping evil memories green. It is at this point that the Confessional makes its most valid claim, for one of its rubrics requires that the penitent pledge himself to refrain from ever discussing again what has once been confessed, either with his confessor or with anyone else. This is wise counsel, as anyone who has been concerned in the cure of souls well knows. And unless all who seek spiritual counsel, whether from a minister or from any trusty friend, are willing to abide by this rule, it were far better if they determined to hid their spiritual wounds from every eye but God's.

IV

The most formidable enemy of the spiritual life, and the last to be conquered, is self-deception; and if there is a better cure for self-deception than silence, it has yet to be discovered. How many of the feverish motions, rooted half in the flesh and half in the nervous system, which we mistake for Divine callings and inspirations would survive the test of silence? We have often been duped by some stirring of surface feeling, or tempermental passion which clothed itself in spiritual garb, when we might have known the truth had we taken our exaltation between our hands, as it were, and put it to the ordeal of silence. What pose, however unconscious, can coexist with habitual silent waiting before God? In nine cases out of ten, the unmasking of spurious vocations and impulses is all that is needed to let the voice of the true Shepherd be heard. That voice is always low and quiet. It often comes in and beneath the calls of ordinary duty. Yet it cannot be mistaken. Only a whisper, but the work is done; a foundation has been laid upon which a new life can be built. Doubt as to the reality of our spiritual experience is our haunting besetment today. From that torture the sensitive among us will never escape, unless we resolve to be still and know.

And here it must be borne in mind that the silence we mean is not self-exploration and self-dissection. Spiritual silence is the turning of the soul in quietness to a Power beyond itself. Self-analysis always breeds either a purely natural excitement—a mere effervescence of high spirits tinged by religious feeling—or else the dullness of self-despair. We are accustomed to defend a purely natural religiosity by way of reaction against the old time orthodoxy which made human nature synonymous with evil. But while human nature is not evil, it is certainly, taken at its highest valuation, the good which is often the worst enemy of the best. Nothing can more effectually frustrate the transmutation of human nature into that which God intends it to be than that same human nature content with its own goodness. For generations we have made war upon a theology which denied the inherent goodness of human nature and made a virtue of self-disparagement. What is the result? Scarcely had we proved, with great satisfaction to ourselves, that the gloomy self-abasement and the grovelling penitence of certain old time saints were due to disordered livers, when laboratory psychology came along and bullied us into believing that spiritual elation was merely natural effervescence plus black coffee, or some less respectable stimulant. So we have come to question the reality of our spiritual exaltation, as we once questioned the reality of other people's spiritual depression. And it is only by the constant, patient effort to attain that stillness in which the voice of God can be heard that we shall ever find rest to our souls. If religion is of any value at all, it must be demonstrable beyond the reach of doubt—as demonstrable as that water wets or fire burns. And it is in the silence that our faith will be spiritually verified.

But how shall we recognize this voice of God, seeing that so many deluding voices call to us in the stillness? To begin with, we must be prepared to find ourselves making mistakes, and not to be discouraged by such mistakes. All life is a pursuit of truth against hazards, and the falsest life of all is that which is forever seeking to guard itself against the risk of imposture. We are sent into the world by the God of brave men that we may, through many mistakes probably, learn to distinguish the voice of the true Shepherd from the voice of "strangers."

The alert and courageous soul making its first venture upon the spiritual life is like a wireless operator on his trial trip in the Pacific. At the mercy of a myriad electrical whispers, the novice at the receiver does not know what to think. How fascinating they are, these ghostly pipings and mutterings, delicate scratchings and thin murmurs—and how confusing! Now he catches the plaintive mutterings of a P. and O. liner trying to reach a French steamer, now the silvery tinkle from a gunboat seeking its shore station. There are aimless but curiously insistent noises, like grains of sand tumbling across tar paper: these are the so-called "static" noises of the atmosphere adjusting itself to a state of electrical balance. Again, there come series of tuneless splashings—that is heat lightning miles away—followed by the rumor of a thunderstorm in the opposite direction. Now he thinks he has got his message, but it is only the murmured greeting of ships that pass in the night. And then, just as his ear has begun to get adjusted to the weird babel of crossing sounds, there comes a remote and thrilling whisper that plucks at his taut nerves and makes him forget all his newly acquired knowledge. It is the singing of the spheres, the electrical turmoil of stars beyond the reach of the telescope, the birth cry and death wail of worlds. And when he is steeped soul deep in the spell of this song of songs, there comes a squeaking, nervous spark, sharp as the squeal of a frightened rat. He decides to ignore it, and then suddenly realizes that it is calling the name of his own boat. It is the expected message, and he nearly missed it.

So the soul that waits in silence must learn to disentangle the voice of God from the net of other voices—the ghostly whisperings of the subconscious self, the luring voices of the world, the hindering voices of misguided friendship, the clamor of personal ambition and vanity, the murmur of self-will, the song of unbridled imagination, the thrilling note of religious romance. To learn to keep one's ear true in so subtle a labyrinth of spiritual sound is indeed as once a great adventure and a liberal education. One hour of such listening may give us a deeper insight into the mysteries of human nature, and a surer instinct for Divine values, than a year's hard study or external intercourse with men. That is why the great solitaries always surprise us by their acute understanding of life. Dwelling apart from men, they none the less have a grasp of human nature which the politician and the financier might envy. They are at home among its intricacies, have plumbed both its meanness and its grandeur, and know how to touch its hidden springs of action. And they know man because they know God and have heard His voice. To know God "preeminently" is their distinction, and it may be ours, at the cost of simple, painstaking honesty with our Maker. Prayer of positive, creative quality needs a background of silence, and until we are prepared to practice this silence, we need not hope to know the power of prayer.

3

The Discipline of Meditation

A little while ago we were told that we had had enough of thinking about God; it was now high time to translate our thinking into practice, mobilize our forces, and "do something." Our young men and women had been captured by the ideal of service, and were only waiting for a Church that would give them something to do and lead them in the doing of it. It sounded plausible, and religious leaders dreamed of a large influx of candidates for the ministry and the Mission Field, not to speak of a host of young lay workers eager to strike out on lines of their own. What actually happened, however, was the reverse of what these sanguine prophets predicted. Not only is there today a tragic scarcity of volunteers for distinctly spiritual work, but even the most broadly humanitarian movements appeal for workers in vain. Why this dearth?

The answer to that question cannot be given in any summary fashion; but there can be no doubt that one of the prime causes for this dearth of volunteers for service, in an age when the idea of service is held in almost superstitious reverence, is simply the lack of clear conceptions of the duty, the motive, and the end of true service. In every department of life we give knowledge its due place. We do not, for instance, put a cricket bat in a boy's hand and pitchfork him into the field without anyone to teach him the rules and "show him how." Yet we have sent a great army of men into life from our Sunday Schools without having given them any more definite kuowledge of religious truth than is held in solution in a vague feeling about God, half instinct, half superstition.

And when we turn from the man in the street to the man in the pew, we find very much the same state of affairs. True, he knows a great deal more about Christianity than his brother outside the Church; but he knows it largely by rote, and as an abstraction out of any close relation to the life he lives and the work he has to do. He knows after a fashion, but he has never been taught to think about what he knows, and to think about it in such a concrete, practical, acutely personal way as to make it truly his own. His prayer life is feeble and intermittent, and his response to the call for service negligible, for the simple reason that he really knows very little at first hand about the God to whom he prays and whom he is called to serve.

Now this may seem as if we were playing with words. Experimental knowledge—the soul's firsthand experience of God—is something other than our intellectual apprehension of Him, and to call both "knowledge" is to mislead. But while there is some truth in this, it must be borne in mind that the two kinds of knowledge are far from unrelated. Experimental knowledge of God may now again come to a thoughtless, careless soul in a flash; but it will not grow, or become vitally influential, unless it be supported and built up by the steady application of the mind to the things by which men live. This does not mean an involved and ambitious intellectual process. The humblest peasant is capable of this steady application, and the restless philosopher, at home in the intricacies of a hundred rival systems, may fail in it completely.

To come to our own case. Behind all true Christian service—service, that is, springing from a sense of Divine vocation and sustained by a supernatural motive—lies the interior life of prayer. And if that prayer life, and therefore the service that springs from it, is feeble and ineffective, it is largely because it lacks the background of genuine, honest thinking. "To think well," says Thomas Traherne, "is to serve God in the interior court." To pray well presupposes patient and systematic meditation; for meditation is nothing else than the art of thinking well and thoroughly upon the truths upon which prayer is based.

Such thinking has little in common with the mere desire for information on religious subjects, or with a talent for discussion; still less does it encourage a taste for controversy. It is the outcome of a settled resolution to come to grips with the great spiritual facts, by pondering them patiently, and painstakingly steeping the mind in them, until it is as completely naturalized in their lofty atmosphere as it is in the air of the market-place. It may well humiliate us to reflect how nimbly, and with what instinctive precision, our minds move among the ordinary actualities of our life in the world, how sensitive they are to every change and how flexible in applying themselves to every new situation, and then to realize how awkward, blunt edged and unadaptable these same minds are when we try to apply them to spiritual reality. There is no shirking the fact that it takes a strict and continuous discipline before the mind becomes tempered to the things of God, sensitive to the tides of grace, and flexible in the hands of the Spirit.

Like all great arts, the art of meditation is not easy, and those who expect their first fumbling attempts to yield a glow and rapture of soul are doomed to disappointment. The road is long and rough, and it is not the hearts of casual and impatient pilgrims that are made to burn as One talks with them by the way. The Christian soldier must make up his mind to endure hardness; it takes sweat of brain and soul before meditation can become a delight. In some cases, indeed, it never becomes delightsome, and yet from that daily half-hour that seems so leaden and dreary, a hidden light will flow into the life.

Much has been written concerning the best methods of meditation, and beginners are distracted by the great multitude of counsellors. A good method is a great help to most people, but in the end each one must discover his own method; and so long as that method includes an act of the will and the affections, and a definite practical resolution—one that can be carried out the same day, if possible—we need not worry unduly over matters of ordeal and detail. The guiding thought that must govern our attempts is that meditation is not reasoning, or quiet musing, or preaching a sermon to ourselves, but a spiritual act as definite and purposeful as a business engagement, a pledge of friendship, or a solemn undertaking. In it we apply spiritual facts and principles to ourselves as individuals and as citizens of the Kingdom of God. We draw out their bearing upon the particular concrete conditions of our own life and its problems. Having pondered them, we seek to appropriate their value by an outgoing of our loving desires toward God, and by exercising our will in the formation of resolutions. A good meditation always issues in a renewal of our vows from some fresh angle; we once again commit ourselves to God, and pledge ourselves to His service under the impulsion of the new thought or insight that has come to us, and in definite relation to the duty of the hour.

It follows that there is no room for ornamental fancy or eloquence in a genuine meditation. It may be profound and intellectually admirable, but even so it must remain quite simple and practical. Whether the person who meditates be a spiritual genius or a dull and poorly endowed soul, the one important question is whether the meditation will stand the wear and tear of common life. If it appears fanciful and visionary, once we have reached the office and plunged into the day's business, it was a failure, no matter how it made our hearts to glow at the time. No meditation is really valid unless it leaves us with something to which we can return during the day's business and find it helpful there. This does not mean, of course, that we must deliberately aim at being dull and obvious in our meditation: what we must aim at is to be natural. If the winged thought and the poetic imagery comes naturally, and—what is of sole importance—if they express vital reality for us, they enhance the value of the meditation. But to seek them is to rob meditation of its true power. If we are indeed bent on facing reality, there is obviously no room for the deliberate culture of charm. The facts of the spiritual life are always beautiful, but their loveliness reveals itself only to the honest eye. They shine in their own light; to see them by the lantern of poetic fancy is to create a mirage.

Perhaps the most common difficulty about meditation is the choice of topic. "With what shall I begin?" is the vexed question, especially for those who come to meditation somewhat late in life. There is only one safe answer. Begin just where you are; that is, with the subject which is of most interest to you at the present stage.

Do we come to meditation as lovers of Nature, who have again and again seen God in some wayside flower? Then let us begin with that flower, seeking to yield ourselves up to the wonderful Life behind it. Like Brother Lawrence, we may become new beings by touching Nature's garment. "He told me," says his biographer, "that in the winter, seeing a tree stripped of its leaves, and considering that within a little time the leaves would be renewed and after that the flowers and fruit appear, he received a high view of the Providence and power of God which has never since been effaced from his soul. This view had set him perfectly loose from the world, and kindled in him such a love for God that he could not tell whether it had increased in above forty years that he had lived since." One might discourse very interestingly about the psychological condition which lay behind this remarkable conversation; but psychology, however important in enabling us to understand our own spiritual adventures, and still more those of other people, helps us very little in making these adventures. What we need is not to become versed in the psychology of the saints, but to get into touch with the objective reality which made them saints. There is a life, a revelation in Nature; and if we humbly and quietly wait upon the power of that life and listen for the voice of the revelation, we shall not be sent empty away. We still like to speak of scientific law. There is no law so scientific as the law that if with all our hearts we truly seek God along the ways that are accessible to us, we shall surely find Him. Communion with God is not an impressionist experience, an incalculable and fugitive emotion. It is based upon the uniformity of the Divine nature, and if we insist upon approaching the quest psychologically, the only psychology we need to concern ourselves with is the psychology of man's response to an eternal and immutable environment.

Or if, perchance, we are lovers of little children and find a whole heaven in a baby's eyes, let us begin our course of meditation by setting a little child—maybe the child we love the best—in the midst of the contending multitude of our thoughts. We are slowly learning that "education" includes the education of parents by their children and of teachers by their pupils, and that the only way to approach a little child rightly is to open one's heart to its unconscious influence, to give oneself to the child in humble, unaffected trustfulness. And as we do this in the spirit of true devotion, we shall discern the mystery and wonder of the Child of Bethlehem. If we have ever really known and loved and studied one little child, we shall never again speak of God as the great "First Cause" and "Architect of the Universe," and think of Him as merely the personification of human progress and destiny. We shall know then that Christianity is the glad tidings of a Savior "wrapped in swaddling clothes, lying in a manger."

II

But if it is well to begin our meditation with the familiar things that have sunk most deeply into our lives, we must beware of ending there. We are all as sheep led by an unknown shepherd, and it is one of our most common fallacies to imagine that that which attracts us most naturally and spontaneously is the thing that corresponds most closely to our deepest needs, and to reject any suggestion of bending our mind to the thing that does not attract as a survival of an irrational asceticism. If the subconscious self means anything, it means that we are not necessarily aware of our deepest and most potent affinities; that what we call our vocation may only be a superficial temperamental inclination, and not the trend of our real nature. The science of the saints anticipated modern psychology in this matter. Again and again the masters of the spiritual life tell us how a call, a vocation, came to them which seemed at first sight entirely uncongenial, and often violently repugnant, to their natural inclination and endowment. But as they followed it patiently and heroically, it became clear that the call that seemed so irrational was addressed to certain intimate susceptibilities and sympathies, and to certain latent capacities and powers, which lay unrecognized in the depth of their being, and would have remained unknown to them had not their brave obedience to the Divine call brought them into conscious activity.

The same holds in the practice of meditation. Subjects which seem uncongenial are often found in the end to answer to an unknown need, and to call forth an unexpected response. There is among us today a universal reluctance to meditate upon the great Christian doctrines—a reluctance which, as we have hinted already, is almost wholly due to the unfortunate circumstance that religious controversy has made us familiar with the objections to these doctrines before we have had time to understand the doctrines themselves. We approach them with a preconceived distaste. We are interested in the revolt of the modern mind against them (forgetting often that there has always been a "modern" mind, and it has always revolted), and seem to find it difficult to realize that the things against which that mind revolts are, to say the least, not uninteresting either Amid the babel of modern pronouncements on the Bible, we forget that the Book has a voice of its own—a message and a power that remain untouched by the passage of time. To listen to that voice and test that power for oneself is well worth all the labor and discipline involved, and to do so one must go to the "great texts." It may be pleasant and soothing to meditate upon the mountain symbolism of the Psalms, or on one of the many humanities in which Scripture abounds; but such meditation will not go far towards enlarging and deepening our minds. What we need is not to muse upon the psychological significance of David's playing on the harp when Saul was in an evil mood, but to ponder on what Jesus meant when He said, "No one knoweth the Father save the Son, and he to whom the Son will reveal Him." We need to wrestle with spiritual principles, to come to grips with the "hard sayings" of the Gospels and the tremendous Pauline paradoxes. Whether our ultimate intellectual conclusions be orthodox or hetero-dox matters comparatively little; the one thing needful is to clear our minds of the small dust of popular controversy and approach the Book "with open face."

And this brings us to the subject of purely topical medi-tation. Nothing can absolve us from applying our minds to the great master facts of the spiritual world—God, Christ, the Holy Spirit, man, sin, grace, death, judgment, the Church Holy and Catholic, the Kingdom that shall have no end. What do we really believe about these facts (what we do not believe about them would probably fill a volume, but is of little real concern, humbling though that fact may be to us), and what is the effect of our belief upon our life? To meditate upon the nature of God is not to construct a theory of the Divine Nature, but to come into vital touch with God Himself through the intelligence. In the course of such a meditation, we shall ask ourselves some searching questions: "What do I really believe about God when I am alone, in my private and secluded heart? What do I believe about Him in times of trouble and crisis? What, in other words, is my working faith—the faith I instinctively apply to the problems of life? How much of the teaching to which I assent as a member of the Church, or of the sentiments I occasionally express in a study circle or other meeting, has really entered into the fiber of my being?"

Such questions, if honestly faced, will take us out of the region of merely individual conviction and experience; for our answers to them will go to prove that while we are fully cognizant of our own difficulties and problems and needs (at least of the more superficial manifestations of them), we really know very little about God at first hand. And at this point our meditation ought to resolve itself into a state of docile attention to the voice of God Himself, a firm resolve to know Him better, and a sincere outgoing of our heart's desire to Him. We become aware at this stage that our conscious difficulties and needs are not the deepest and most real, and we shall feel impelled to turn from our known selves to Him "to whom all hearts are open, all desires known, and from whom no secrets are hid"—the God who searches and interprets the subconscious self. We shall feel that there are in God whole worlds of grace and glory which have not entered into our personal experience, but which are none the less of supreme moment to us, both as individuals and as members of God's family; and if we are wise, we shall gird ourselves to explore these unknown tracts, for they will prove to be "our own country."

The task is not an easy one. At first we shall grope and stumble along a path lit but dimly and fitfully. Distractions—the chronic torment of those who wish to meditate—will drag us back at every step, and we shall often lose heart. But while we need to be severe with those recalcitrant minds of ours that are always going off at a tangent, we also need to remember that Christian meditation is not a New Thought drill in concentration or self-hypnotism. Distractions need not be hindrances. They may be, and often are, the raw material of a far more profitable meditation than the one they interrupt. If, during a meditation upon God, the thought of some harassing care or absorbing occupation recurs again and again, why not make that thought part of the meditation by seeking to learn how the spiritual fact we are pondering bears upon it? After all, the first requirement of a good meditation is not flawless logical sequence, but *reality;* and many a so-called distraction is nothing else than the voice of God recalling us from mere speculation to reality. But while meditation must be related to personal problems, it must never be allowed to spell either self-introspection or absorption in one's own problems. Self-regard is the slum of the soul, and the supreme function of meditation is to lift us out of its squalor into the clear, pure air of the spiritual world.

III

In meditation God grows upon us until we are saturated with the thought of Him. At first the whole spiritual world seems a vague abstraction, but gradually, as we gaze with reverent, steadfast eyes into that infinite Life from which we came and from whose exhaustless fountain the frail vessels of our lives are filled, we come to discern its beauty and splendor. What was vague and empty is seen to be a full and wonderfully articulated reality. Gradually but surely, we become "familiar with the infinite riches of the many-sided idea which is God."

Perhaps it is the mystery of Creation that first enthralls us. Of a sudden—we know not how, but we know it came by habit of fixed attention—we see creation as a romance, the wooing of the Eternal Lover. We discern the self-giving Love in the heart of God when He made man. We see it take flesh in Jesus. How shall we name Him who is the Fountain of Love, and Him in whom the Response of Love became incarnate, and Him who is the Tide of Love sweeping from God to man and from man back to God? What if, after all, the great Catholic insight into the mystery of Love which we call the doctrine of the Trinity holds that truth which alone can satisfy and build up our souls?

In something after this fashion, we may, through meditation, rediscover for ourselves the truths about God which some like to call dogma, but which are in reality seeds of life. It will come to us that what theologians call the Incarnation means a revolutionary reorganization of humanity. Where before we relegated it to the region of dry doctrine, we find now that is a principle whose implications extend over the whole of the world's life. We realize that it pledges each of us to a way of life so new and wonderful that we shrink from its mingled glory and terror, while leaping to its thrilling challenge—a way of life so broad that it embraces the whole universe, and yet so narrow that there is no room in it for even a halfstarved self. We also gain glimpses into the mystery of the Spirit's working. The Dove that hovered over the waters of Christ's baptism, the Pentecostal tongues of fire, the power that created the Body of Christ which is the Church become symbols of a living reality to be progressively appropriated in experience.

The Gospel story, which has become mere history—and legendary history at that—for so many of us now reveals its timeless value. Gazing upon Jesus in humble, loving meditation, we shall see the uncreated Life clothing itself with our human nature, and taking the flickering torch of our mortality into its deathless glow.

The nativity and childhood, the baptism, the temptation, the three years' ministry, and the passion and death of Jesus yield up their compelling significance to our waiting souls. We no longer see them, with dull eyes, as mere stages in the development of the greatest among the sons of men, but as freed from the "wheel of becoming," and taking their place in the world of eternal fact. Each shines for us with its own creative light, for from each there streams out a restoring and transforming energy such as can reside in no mere historical happening. Hampered no longer by the importunate irrelevancies of theoretical discussion, we adore the Child Jesus with the shepherds of Bethlehem, and so learn the secret to which mere investigation, whether its results be orthodox or heterodox, has no key. We know why the sages worshipped "when they saw the young Child with Mary His mother."

Each successive movement in the drama of our redemption appears in its own perfection, and communicates its own gifts to our souls. Each makes its own demands, and suggests its own method of approach. The contemplation of the Nativity initiates us into the path of humility. The stages of the three years' ministry impose their appropriate spiritual discipline upon us. The redeeming death reveals to us the pearl of penitence, and exercises us in the theology of the broken and contrite heart. We shall not close our eyes to critical values; but we shall give to critical inquiry its own place, which is a more important one than traditionalists dream of, and a less important one than modernists like to think.

We shall find that as we go on, our meditations, instead of growing more elaborate and complex, will grow steadily simpler, one single thought often sufficing to fill the time. F. W. Faber has well said that one commonplace truth which would seem tame and trivial to the beginner suffices a saint for hours of contemplation. We have often marvelled how simple, how childish almost, are the recorded devotions and aspirations of many of the mightiest spirits, and in what reverence they held certain books which we cast aside as quite too elementary and commonplace for our color-loving minds. But as we go on in the lowly way of meditation, we too shall become capable of that "loving, simple, sustained attention of the mind to divine things," which sees "a whole world in a grain of sand." That steadfast spiritual gaze and loving adherence of the soul to God which caused St. Francis to find food for lifelong meditation in the one phrase, "My God and my All," is not a negation of the intellect, an artificial return to childish ways. It is rather an intellectual achievement (where intellect means not mere reasoning, but the exercise of the larger reason which includes spiritual imagination), akin to that of the scientist who can take in a large group of facts at one simple glance, and almost instinctively synthesize them into a single unity. It belongs to the realm of that spiritual intelligence which is the very flower of thinking and reasoning. Nothing reveals the essential vulgarity of the restless impressionist mind more than the things that tire and bore it. In this sense, also, to love God with the brooding love that finds its absorbing occupation in the mere gazing upon the Beloved is a liberal education.

IV

We are thus led by the practice of meditation from the point where self occupies the center of our thought and we expect God "to revolve diligently round us," to the point where we become predominantly aware of God. We are now far more concerned about the claims of the love of God upon us than about even the most spiritual of our own moods and desires. God is becoming the central reality— the beginning, middle and end of our prayer. All men have the power of seeing God and realizing His presence spasmodically and in flashes, but the spiritual discipline of meditation raises what was an evanescent mood to a sustained habit.

If, then, we have been faithful in our meditation and not allowed it to become an occasion of self-seeking, we shall find that love to God—that steady and profound gravitation towards our Creator and Redeemer which is more than an emotion, and in which lies our very life—will be born in the heart. Who can compel love? we often ask; and how can we, whose spirits blow where they list, obey a command to love the Unseen? In meditation we may find an answer. We love God so little because we know Him so imperfectly. Who loves a chance acquaintance? "We know and have believed," says St. John, "the love of God towards us."

The unknown may, and does, exert an initial attraction; but our response depends upon our knowledge. In valid meditation that knowledge dawns and grows. Thoughts come to us which are no mere intellectual apprehensions, but lay compelling hands upon emotion and will. Through them the love of God is shed abroad in our hearts, and ere we know it we respond in some measure. We must needs love, since He has first loved us. There is but one love, and it created as well as recreated us. To be made in God's image is to be made to love Him, and to love Him means life from the dead. The humblest act, then, becomes an offering of love—radiant, beautiful, exquisite as no work of art can be exquisite. Each word becomes mystical and holy because it is the impulse of love articulate. The meditation which does not waken love in our hearts, however poor and feeble that beginning of love may be, is imperfect; for where God and the soul really meet, there the intelligence, the will, and the emotions rise together, and what before was hearsay of conventional theology becomes self-evident truth. God reveals Himself as the supremely loving and lovable One; and love, as Thomas Traherne reminds us, is continually communicating, propagating, and begetting itself.

We see now how far astray we are when we speak of the burning love of the saints for God as a mediæval characteristic impossible to men of our day. The love of man for God is not the fashion of any age. It is grounded beyond the reach of change in the nature of God and man. Its expression varies from age to age, but its power persists unweakened; and the last lesson which the last man born on this earth must learn is that man's sole dignity and happiness lies in learning to love his Maker and to serve Him out of pure love. The difference between the saints of old and ourselves is not one of inherent nature: it is simply that they took time to ponder God, to gaze upon Him in an act of supreme attention in which intelligent will and desire concurred in perfect harmony, while we are too greatly overrun with small activities and occupations to find leisure for such pondering. No human being, whether living in the earliest ages of desert spirituality, or in the foremost files of our time, who has really set himself to live in the thought of God but has felt the glow of a new affection, the unsealing of a fountain of love within.

And as we ponder and are silent, that Love will utter its unspoken demands. In some form or other, we shall hear the cry, "My son, give me thy heart." And on our answer to that cry hangs our destiny.

4

From Self to God

In defining the essence of prayer as the soul's loving intercourse with God, and its primary condition as detachment from self and attachment to the Divine Friend, we seem to lay ourselves open to the objection that such intercourse issues in a dreamy mysticism, and results in a view of life which reduces the world to "a garden seat whereon the soul may make love to God." Life becomes a *solitude à deux*, and pious absorption in God proves to be as selfish an affair as romantic absorption in a beloved human.

The validity of this objection depends entirely, however, upon the conception of God which is involved. If God is seen merely as the great Other, the soul's Divine Counterpart; if, in short, our attachment to Him is conceived of in terms of romance, then prayer must logically lead us into a cloistered and somewhat sickly pietism out of relation to the world and its needs. But so to conceive of God is to hold converse with a phantom. God is not merely the mystic Lover: He is the center of a whole world of eternal reality, and prayer involves the soul's discovery of that world and its progressive adjustment to its new environment. This implies activity of the highest order—activity in which mind, will, and emotion work together at their highest potency. If, further, we define God as creative and redeeming Love, His world of reality becomes the scene of His creative and

63

redemptive activity; and prayer, so far from alienating us from humanity, will give us a new understanding of it, and a new concern for its destiny. It will commit us to take our share in the plan and purpose of a God who so loved the world that He gave Himself for its redeeming. As we pray we shall, like George Fox, be "baptized into a sense of the conditions and needs of all men."

I

But while creative prayer must result in a passion for humanity, it must begin with a single eye towards God. At the beginning of our prayer life we are self-centered. Prayer means little more to us than "asking." We ask for personal favors, for blessings upon ourselves and those belonging to us. In our prayer vocabulary personal pronouns occupy a disproportionate place. It is *my* needs, *my* relations, *my* friends; and even when we go further afield and pray for those whom we have never seen, it is because their needs have been so presented to us as to stir our sympathies and appeal to our idiosyncrasies. In the last resort, we still make use of God in prayer. What altruism we have is temperamental, and remains uninformed by a deep view of God and man, and limited by our natural affinities; our prayer, in fact, remains essentially self-centered. And it belongs to the pathos of our spiritual pilgrimage that so many sincere and noble souls never seem to get beyond the prayer of self-regard and self-reference.

Moreover, many of the new methods of prayer which profess to deliver us from the prison house of self are seen, upon closer analysis, to be but subtle variations of the self-centered prayer. Not a few leaders of fashionable prayer cults make a point of insisting on complete concentration upon God as the prime condition of success. Human need, they urge, must be forgotten entirely. The devotee must, by intense mental abstraction and concentration, ascend to heavenly places, and think only of God in His inalienable omnipotence, indestructible peace, and inextinguishable joy. Only so shall His victorious and health-giving power be communicated to us, and through us to those for whom we pray. But all the time the motive of this "giving out of one-self into God" is to gain relief from trouble, sickness, or sin. No less than frankly self-centered prayer, these cults make God not an end, but a means to an end. They name God, and intend self.

But in the normal course of our spiritual growth, there comes a time when the center of prayer shifts from self to God. Petition, in its narrower sense, recedes. True, it is not excluded, for nothing that touches us can be indifferent to our Father in Heaven; and our Lord Himself had a special love for plain, forthright, "unmystical" folk, who asked God for what they wanted, as simply and frankly as they would ask their neighbor to help them out in a domestic emergency. But petition will no longer be the pivot upon which prayer turns. The true motive power will now be to get nearer God, to know Him better, to experience His friendship, to enter more fully into His thoughts and purposes.

Self-centered prayer leaves us exposed to a thousand doubts and fears. Experience gives the lie to theory, and the sense of blessings withheld and requests ungranted lays a choking hand upon faith. We know not how to answer the skeptic who reminds us that his child, for whom he did not pray, recovered, while ours died. Books fail to reassure us, and we wonder if prayer is, after all, no more than a process of autosuggestion. And all the time it is our fundamental attitude that is at fault. Prayer is simply intelligent, purposeful, devoted contact with God. Where that contact is established and sustained, prayer will "work" infallibly, according to its own inherent laws. But such contact cannot be established until we see God as the center of an eternal world of love in which we have citizen rights and duties, and until we act upon that vision. Failing this, the contact remains partial and spasmodic, and prayer, so far from justifying itself, needs to be bolstered up by a hundred arguments, none of which succeeds in convincing even the apologist himself.

We need devise no elaborate theory or method of God-centered prayer. There is only one "rubric"—*the lifting up to God of our honest desire to know Him and to be made one with Him*. God conscious prayer at its highest involves honest thinking, and a firm resolution to bring all our problems to the searchlight of His truth and to submit all our work to the touchstone of His interests and intentions. A lifelong discipline—intellectual, spiritual, and moral—is needed before we can call ourselves adepts in creative prayer. Yet the least gifted and most poorly equipped soul can attain mastery in it; for, from first to last, simple, honest desire for the love and fellowship of God is the "chief priest" of all its mysteries.

II

God-centered prayer, then, means to enter the world of reality. It may be defined as a progressive revaluation of the whole of life in accordance with a revolutionary experience which we have called the shifting of centers; but it is far better to approach it more simply, and conceive of it as a living way—the way of Love. For that world of reality of which God is the center is the world of enduring and victorious Love, and its highway—the great orientating path that gives it coherence—is Christ. "Thy life is our way," says Thomas à Kempis; and the life of Christ in its eternal significance is indeed at once the way which each individual disciple has to tread, and the way of God in human history.

We are here in the region of that mystical "Christ process"—the recapitulation of the birth, life, and death of Christ by the individual soul—which seems so remote and confusing to the plain man, largely because its exponents have clothed it in a difficult and esoteric jargon. But, in reality, it is quite simple—difficult, indeed, as all great things are difficult, but never remote from life or inaccessible to the average intelligence. It means that Christ did not come merely to be our Example or our Guide, but to live a new kind of human life, and to live it in such a way that each of us can live it after Him in individual fashion. His life—the new order of living which He initiated—is a way, a path, the key to a new world. It can only be understood by living it after Him; to view it externally is to miss it altogether.

> *Were Christ a thousand times in Bethlehem born*
>   But not in thee,
> *Still wert thou all forlorn!*

We know that is true. We may say that there is nothing mystical about it, that it simply means that we must have the spirit of Christ; but what could be more mystical than having this spirit of Christ—what more mystical, indeed, than the birth of love of whatever kind within the soul? How is this spirit possessed? The intellect cannot convey it to the life; mere willing cannot conjure it from the eternal deeps; burning emotion cannot fix it into our nature as an enduring principle. Proximity to Christ, whether literal or mental, cannot give it to man; else Judas Iscariot must have possessed it, and every theologian be a saint. To say that it comes by prayer, by the lifting up of a humble heart to God, is to say the most mystical thing of all.

It is to affirm that prayer is supernatural. We shrink from the term "supernatural," and it may be conceded at once that what we have called the supernatural life of prayer is truly natural, if Nature be taken to include the Divine-Human as incarnate in Christ. But just as human thought and emotion are "supernatural" with reference to the brute creation, so the life of creative prayer is supernatural in regard to the life we conventionally term human. Its impulse and sustaining power come from beyond man. It is a Divine mystery—the mystery of the birth and life, the dying and rising again, of Christ, recapitulated in the soul that prays. We need not describe this mystery in high-sounding terms; each event represents a stage in the process of the shifting of centers, the pilgrimage of the soul from itself to God.

Let us seek to trace this Way, which is Christ. Assuming that we have had some experience of self-centered prayer— genuine and fruitful as far as it went, yet essentially self-regarding—there comes a time when this way of prayer no longer suffices. The awakening may come through the intellect, or through the deeper emotions. It may be a sharp pain, or only a dull uneasiness. In any case, we feel the stirring of that buried life in the deeps below consciousness—the life that lies at once beyond and at the back of reason and will, unrecognized by us, yet capable of using our faculties. The discovery of this hidden element in our being may at first lead to nothing more than a revolt against institutional religion. We feel unsatisfied with what churches and religious systems have to offer. These things do not meet our new needs; the remedies they possess do not touch the aching nerve of our being. At this stage we shall be tempted to turn from organized forms of spirituality, and to seek refuge from the repugnances of the corporate Body of Christ in the solitude of our own spirits. In this there is danger, however. It is but a plausible version of the Satanic temptation, "If thou be the Son of God, cast thyself down, for he shall give his angels charge concerning thee." Our safety lies, not in separation, but in loyalty. It is precisely when the Church appears to have least to offer us, that our wisdom lies most surely in remaining within her courts; for we may be certain that the soul that finds nothing but emptiness within the collective experience and life of believers will find nothing but hallucination and delusion within its solitary self.

In such hours we need the utmost self-restraint, and the most humble attention to the voice of God. We do not know what is being wrought in us; we cannot see the Holy Thing that will surely be brought to birth, if only we say from our hearts, "Be it unto me according to thy word." All we are conscious of is restlessness, dissatisfaction, peevishness. The house of selfhood is being demolished over our heads. What satisfied us before inspires us now with weariness and distaste. The shell of natural religiousness has cracked, and our unloveliness obtrudes. We are drawn to pray in the

Spirit, but realize that there can be no "my" or "mine" in such prayer, whereas we are full of "my" and "mine." It is a period of painful incubation which may be spoiled by a single touch of self-will. Nothing avails here but perfect docility. A demand is being made upon us—the demand for obedience, and for that royal generosity which gives all for all, asking nothing back—and our response to that demand will depend upon our willingness to cease from self, and upon our loyalty to that deeper life whose stirrings we can only half understand.

III

Then, perhaps by a sudden, sharp invasion of a new life flooding ours from without, as it were, or by the sudden rising of the flood from within the deeps of the spirit—probably by the meeting of both—we become conscious of the birth of the Christ spirit within ourselves, and of our own birth into a new and wonderful world. Or the process may be of the most gentle and almost imperceptible nature. A brooding stillness about us, the coming of light we know not how, the sacramental renewal of soul by an element that dropped upon it as silently as manna, and in as impenetrable a night of obscurity—in these, and in countless other ways, some of them inexpressible in words, the new life comes. But however it comes, it means the soul's emergence into a world familiar yet almost frighteningly unfamiliar—a world in which we feel utterly strange and awkward, and which we yet recognize as our true home.

It is the world of which God is the center. We look upon Him, and our life is renewed. We are given a set of new values, a spiritual coinage other than that with which we have hitherto traded. Things that but a little while ago seemed desirable now appear as dross. Things we recently dubbed "queer" and fanciful suddenly become entirely natural and solidly substantial. We discover untold beauties in God; we find in Christ secrets of final restitution that fill us with deathless hope. Matter is seen to be the store-house of unguessed spiritual treasure, a hiding place of holy powers, a laboratory of Divine alchemy. Everywhere we see mysteries of healing and regeneration, of individual transfiguration and of world renewal that remained hidden while self was our center. And as these revelations unfold themselves, the world we once lived in appears as a shrivelled shell, a mere travesty of reality mocking us with its pathetic makeshifts for power and joy. We have become dead to a whole universe of delights and sorrows, and alive to an entirely different range of thoughts and emotions. It is as though we had developed a new set of faculties of appreciation and distaste, pleasure, and pain.

While our birth into the new world is full of Bethlehem joys, it also, like Bethlehem, involves a sword that shall pierce us through. Every genuine experience of new life in Christ has this in common with the sterile extravagances of religious self-delusion: that both excite the ridicule and opposition of the worldly and of the merely conventionally religious. Both beget a sense of loneliness, and plunge the soul, fresh from the glow and rhythm of its rapture, into the chilling waters of petty criticism. And it is the manner in which we meet this check to our new found joy that proves the validity or otherwise of our experience. The soul that has passed through a merely aesthetic and emotional process will either be betrayed into hostility against its critics, or it may take refuge in the calm contempt of the artist for the Philistine, wrapping itself in its own sensations and ignoring the jibes of the vulgar herd.

But he in whom the Christ has been born knows neither resentment nor contempt. So far from allowing his spiritual experience to alienate him from his brethren, he sees in their misunderstanding of him an added claim upon his sympathy. For as Christ was born into the world, not to stand apart from the common life of man as a judge, but to share it as a brother, subjecting Himself joyfully to all the limitations and pains such a fellowship involved, so he in whom Christ's spirit dwells will steadfastly refuse any form of religious or mystical exaltation that releases him from the hampering influence of common relationships. The dull-souled who sneer and jibe at him, and the ill-willed who meet him with anger and malice, will have no judge more lenient, no interpreter more sympathetic, than the subject of their ridicule or enmity. At the very threshold of a sharply individual experience, the soul that is truly submitted to God will realize its oneness with all men. It is not a question of cultivating the corporate feeling, as if it were something superadded to a man's experience of Christ.

God sees us not merely as individuals, but also in an ideal relation to our fellows; and as the love of God is shed abroad in our hearts, we shall freely and generously identify ourselves with the weakest and most wayward, bearing their burdens and taking them into the very center of our prayers. The self-deluded soul goes forth in search of a spiritual romance, an emotional adventure that exalts it above other souls; but the soul in whose depths Christ is truly born covets no spiritual privileges that make for isolation, refusing to be made perfect without its fellows. Here is the final test of religious experience. No matter how glorious the soul's adventure be, whether in the realm of mystic feeling or intellectual apprehension, if it does not mean a passing out of self into that life of God which is world-embracing love, it is nothing, and worse than nothing. When we adopt the language of the mystics and represent the soul's pilgrimage as a "recapitulation" of the life of its Lord, we do so because that life was fundamentally a surrender of self, and each event in it a stage in the process of deepening surrender.

Mystics have erred in treating of the Christ process as if it exhausted all spiritual experience, instead of representing only one of several ways of symbolizing that experience, and also in applying the events of our Lord's life in rigid sequence and pedantic detail to the life of the soul. Needless to say, such a procedure is artificial, and calculated to prejudice sensible people. There are as many ways of recapitulating Christ as there are souls. To some the Transfiguration, for instance, will become a center of experience, leaving its mark upon the whole life. Others will, at some great crisis of their lives, be remade by the reality embodied in our Lord's Temptation in the wilderness. One will appropriate the mystery of Cana, and find the secret that turns all life's water to wine; another will be initiated into the sacrament of the baptism in Jordan. Some find nearly every event of Christ's life reflected in their experience; while many more can trace no such detailed correspondence, and yet are able to say with St. Paul that they were crucified with Christ and are risen again with Him. The one universal element which pervades all experience is the emergence of a new life, with standards and values of its own, involving a progressive discipline, in which the self-principle is slowly put to death, and God becomes the center of the whole life.

As we become naturalized in the world of Divine reality, we shall be surprised to find that, instead of an ever increasing fervor and delight in communion with God, our prayer life will sooner or later be characterized by "dryness" and depression. We shall cease to feel the presence of God. Our quiet hours will become disconcertingly bleak, and barren of tangible result. Our meditations will be unfruitful, blighted by distraction and poverty of thought. Prayer will die on our lips, and we shall lose all sense of contact with God. If we have been accustomed to regard a sense of joy and exaltation, and an abiding consciousness of communion with God, as the test of a genuine prayer life, we shall feel that we have been deceived in ourselves, and be tempted to give up the quest.

Three-fourths of our difficulties about prayer in its most spiritual aspect would disappear, if we realized the simple truth that prayer is a dying to self and becoming alive unto God, and that each stage of a progressive prayer life is a stage in the putting to death of the self that God may work and reign. The stages may be many and subtle, or few and clearly observable by all; in any case, they will be recognizable as so many aspects of God's holy war against self-love. At the beginning, when prayer is still in its self-centered stage, we cling to material pursuits and pleasures. Then comes the birth of Christ in us, and we are weaned from these delights by the inrush of spiritual joys. A new range of pleasures has become ours, and our former delights appear dull and worthless. And in our absorption in the delights of the spirit, we imagine that we have left self behind for ever.

But self is not dead: it has merely lost consciousness of its existence for a season, in its absorption in a new object of desire. It clings to its spiritual treasure as it once clung to the goods of earth. It is only when God withdraws these spiritual possessions from us that we realize how largely self entered into our holding of them. One by one they leave us —the first joy and fervor, the first well-nigh intoxicating sense of God's presence, the first inrush of unconquerable might and dauntless confidence. They are taken from us, not harshly, but to make room for something less vivid and joyous, yet even more solidly sustaining—a deep, calm peace, a sense of perfect rest in God. We find, as we go on, that this new stillness of peace has a charm all its own. It, no less than the exuberance of joy, is a luxury. How gladly we let ourselves sink into its depths!

But again it is self-love that hugs this peace of God to its arms, and we never really become aware of the depth of our self-love until God begins to tear it out of our hearts. Now peace, in its turn, is taken away from us, and we go forth into an arid wilderness. Our spiritual imagination fails, our feeling is numbed, words forsake us, thought is clogged, our spirits faint within us, and the heart is left cold as last year's nests. We know not what to do. We have lost, not only self-confidence, but self-resource. God has withdrawn His hand, and we are left desolate. It is at this stage that the temptation to turn back and renounce the pilgrim's habit becomes a real danger. At other stages this temptation arises from fickleness; it is but one mood among many. Now it springs from a vision of grim reality. For the first time we see ourselves as we are apart from God— naked, impotent, dead. At last we know that we can find no rest in self; and God—how far away God has withdrawn

Himself! But this hour that seems so evil is the hour of our salvation. In it, as in nothing that has gone before, God is surrounding us with the purifying and healing energies of love.

Our greed for that sensible warmth of religious feeling miscalled "experience" in some quarters is one of our most dangerous enemies. We constantly hark back to the radiant happiness of the early Christians, point to the palpable gladness that throbs through the Apostolic narrative, and say that spiritual life must be like that; if we lack joy, we lack God. But we forget that joy does not come by seeking it. To the early Christians, who embraced God with perfect simplicity, asking no questions, giving not a look behind them, and selling the whole field of the world for the pearl of great price, joy came immediately; for joy is the reward of complete surrender, and God never keeps one waiting unduly. But we, hesitant, sophisticated, torn between rival theories and allegiances, making a study of self-analysis and self-expression, do not, as a rule, make this complete surrender until, by pain and desolation, the heart has been purged of its idols and the roots of self-love cut out of the soul. It is then, and only then, that joy can come. The way to it may be long and hard, but the moment the last step is taken and the life wholly yielded up to God, joy such as we have never known—radiant, triumphant, immutable —becomes ours.

V

It is not easy for us to believe this, for we are slow to relinquish the notion that prayer is a form of spiritual enjoyment, or at least a source of spiritual satisfaction. We do not realize that while a vivid consciousness of God, a flood of spiritual joy, the touch of inspiration and the flame of fervor are all valid and desirable elements of prayer, they are not of its essence—they are certainly not its central object. Some of the most profound spiritual writers go so far as to confine them to the immature stages of prayer. They are the marks of the neophyte in Christ—the sugarplums awaiting spiritual babes to tempt them to take the first step. While we need not concur in a judgment which is not borne out by Christian experience, we shall do well to recognize that vivid emotion in prayer is one of the most fruitful sources of self-deception and therefore one of the most formidable hindrance to true progress.

For prayer, we must remember, is, first and foremost, an act of devotion; and devotion is not an affair of fervid feeling or tender sentiment, but a solemn act, whereby a man devotes, commits, consecrates himself wholly to God. Now, if such consecration means anything, it means the death of that self-will and self-love which separate the soul from its true Source; and that type of prayer is surely best which most effectually mortifies our lower self. And no one who has had any experience of the spiritual life would care to maintain that prayer which is accompanied by a feeling of intense satisfaction and emotion is the most likely to purge us of self-love. On the contrary, the danger of such prayer is that it gives self-love a unique opportunity. Self feeds on emotional prayer, and gradually we forget that we are *in via*—on pilgrimage from self to God—and that we are making no progress unless prayer becomes increasingly a fight to the death between the self that battens upon emotional luxury and the love that claims that self as a living sacrifice. The central thing in prayer is not the garden of the soul, but the altar of dedication. If we can go to that altar with joy and singing, happy are we; but more blessed are those who ascend its steps in the nakedness of faith, giving all for all and asking nothing in return, save that the will of God may be fulfilled in them.

It is well therefore that after we have made the great dedication, we should be led into that arid twilight land where our schemes miscarry and our judgments mislead us, where emotion withers and will is seen to be but a broken reed, where we grope and totter and fall until we realize how frail was the staff of self upon which we had leaned, and, mistrusting ourselves, learn to put all our confidence in God. For the end He has in view for us is not our straitening, but our enlargement. We are stripped of self-resource, not that we might be humiliated, but that we might discover the unguessed resources we have in God. It is not the reflex influence of "dry" prayer in making us wiser and sadder men that is its central significance, but its revelation of God as the one true life. If true prayer, so far from being a luxury, is one long crucifixion (as Père Caussade has it), it is with Christ we are crucified, that we might live with Him and He in us. We give thanks for "dry" prayer, not because there is any virtue in "dryness" or dullness, but because in it we are stripped from delusion in order that we might possess the supreme Reality.

So far, then, from being a crushing and narrowing experience, his "dryness" in prayer, with its revelation of the supremacy of God, is a great emancipation. We emerge from it as God's freemen. We are no longer the slaves of our devotional moods, our religious prejudices and predilections.

Ambition no longer tempts us; human judgment ceases to intimidate us. We are delivered from the disabling fear of failure. Raised above the attractions and inhibitions of conventional religion, we partake, in some measure, of the glorious immutability of God Himself. Our wills are tempered to steel. It was said of the early Jesuits that "when once the saints of the Society said, *I will,* the thing was done"; and it has always been true of those whose strength was rooted in the Cross, where self had been crucified with Christ.

And if a will of iron represents one aspect of the liberated soul, flexibility and detachment of spirit represent a complementary aspect. To obey the inspirations of grace moment by moment, to adjust oneself readily to the promptings of a living Master, is a task which demands the glorious liberty that is the high prerogative of the sons of God. Complete docility to the Divine Guide, instant response to His most fragmentary suggestions, and unhesitating readiness to go where He sends us, even though the call of today seems to contradict the command of yesterday—such flexibility presupposes a royal heart of devotion which defies human canons of consistency and looks to God only. Such a heart is not born in a man until he has been in that dark and secret place where he dies to self that he may live to God.

St. Philip Neri will always remain the classic example of this superb courage of obedience. He had no set rules or methods, no religious peculiarity of his own. He joined no monastic Order, and would have no vows in the Congregation which he founded. He had no "views," made few plans, and was ready to give up what he was doing at any moment. In fine, he took no thought for his spiritual career, but simply exposed himself to God's action upon him day after day, not in an attitude of sterile quietism, but in the spirit of joyous cooperation. And it is little to be wondered at that this quiet, jocund, free and easy man, who was so careless about "giving edification," and so utterly detached from everything that was a means and not an end, exercised an almost irresistible attraction over his contemporaries, winning them from sin and worldliness, subduing their lusts, calming their fears, moulding them to Christian ways, entering into their lives with the transforming ministries of the Gospel, as noiselessly and naturally as the sunlight enters a window at dawn.

The man who is freed from self and has found his true life in God is free indeed. He is untroubled by anxiety even about the affairs of the Kingdom of God. He is never hurried, does not seek place and power, is patient with himself as with others, and takes his faults and failures quietly. There is nothing showy or theatrical about such a man. His life is hid with Christ in God, and hidden from no one more than from himself. Coventry Patmore has given us an inimitable portrait of such a man:

The saint has no "fads," and you may live in the same house with him and never find out that he is not a sinner like yourself, unless you rely on negative proofs, or obtrude lax ideas upon him and so provoke him to silence. He may impress you, indeed, by his harmlessness and imperturbable good temper, and probably by some lack of appreciation of modern humor, and ignorance of some things which men are expected to know, and by never seeming to have much use for his time when it can be of any service to you; but on *the whole, he will give you an agreeable impression of general inferiority to yourself. You must not, however, presume upon this inferiority so far as to offer him any affront, for he will be sure to answer you with some quiet and unexpected remark, showing a presence of mind—arising, I suppose, from the presence of God—which will make you feel that you have struck rock and only shaken your own shoulder. If you compel him to speak about religion, . . . he will most likely dwell with reiteration on commonplaces which you were perfectly well acquainted before you were twelve years old; but you must make allowance for him, and remember that the knowledge which is to you a surface is to him a solid. . . . I have known two or three such persons, and I declare that, but for the peculiar line of psychological research to which I am addicted, and hints from others in some degree akin to these men, I should never have guessed that they were any wiser or better than myself, or any other ordinary man of the world with a prudent regard for the common proprieties. I once asked a person, more learned than I am in such matters, to tell me what was the real difference. The reply was that the saint does everything that any other decent person does, only somewhat better and with a totally different motive.**

The spirit of hiddenness, which, as has well been said, is three-fourths of Christianity, and the grace of doing common things in a supernatural way—these are the marks of the man who has been created anew, and prayer which does not stamp these marks upon the soul is greatly to be suspected.

* *The Rod, the Root, and the Flower, pp. 160-162*

VI

And here we come to the heart of our subject. To have passed from self to God means to possess the spirit that does everything for the pure love of God—the spirit that made God as real to Brother Lawrence among his pots and pans in the kitchen as on his knees before the Blessed Sacrament. It transmutes every action into an offering of love, makes of every homely gesture an act of pure worship. In reading such a record as that of Brother Lawrence, we are struck by the simplicity of his religion. He has no theology, no elaborate ethic, no method of self-discipline; his only doctrine is the doctrine of doing one's daily work, even to the picking up of a straw from the floor, with a motive of love to God and as an act of devotion. It appeals to our preference for an undogmatic Christianity, and to our sense of the sacredness of what men call secular. It is such a practical faith, we say, so well within the reach of everybody. But when we come to practice it, we find that its simplicity existed only in our imagination. It is quite easy to believe that there is no limit to the creative power of one homely act of service done for the love of God, that it contains sufficient dynamic to break the whole life in pieces and make it anew after a Divine pattern. We believe it because we have seen reflections of this glory in the most unlikely places. We have seen a poor seamstress, for instance, stitching away at her ill paid labor in sullen resentment and dull defiance, and then seen her stitching away even more busily for her little child, and we have bowed before the omnipotence of transmuting love which can change leaden toil to golden delight at one touch. But when we come to practice the presence of God after the manner of Brother Lawrence,* we find it an impossible business. Surely there is a flaw somewhere. Whatever may have been true of Brother Lawrence's time, we cannot solve the problem of life after this fashion, cannot acquiesce in degrading work or unjust conditions of labor for the love of God. If we are fellow workers with God, we demand in His name the right to tasks worthy of His partners.

There are two reasons for the difficulty we experience in translating the golden precept of Brother Lawrence into terms of present day life. To begin with, we are so deeply imbued with the modern ideas of self-expression that we cannot acquiesce in uncongenial work and hampering conditions. And while our discontent may not be wrong, its motive certainly is. If we are to rebel against our work, it must be, not because that work does not express ourselves, but because it does not express what we believe to be God's thought and will for us. We must choose between the ideal of self-expression and the ideal of vocation—the call to express God. The collision between the two ideals is sharp and radical, and it seems at first sight as if to surrender our right to self-expression were to stultify the humanity which God has given us. But a deeper view resolves the contradiction. Who, for instance, is the true artist—he who goes to Nature to use her as a means of self-expression, or he who approaches her as a humble servant, seeking to record a fragment of her creative profusion simply because the truth of her is so beautiful? Who is the great writer— he who looks to his writing as a means of making him famous, or he who loses all personal ambition in his desire

---

* *Brother Lawrence* a Forward Movement Booklet, 35 cents per copy.

to interpret life simply because of his reverence and love for it? The answer is obvious. And the same holds true in the spiritual life. The true master is he who is so bent upon his art—the loving realization of God in terms of life—that he forgets the medium.

But a deeper reason for our difficulty is found in the fact that there is no merit whatsoever in choosing uncongenial work, or in persevering in it, unless that work really be our vocation. Most of those who quote Brother Lawrence miss this point. They seem to think that what he intended to teach was that any and every kind of work we happened to be engaged in was to be continued with a new motive; that the secret of possessing God was simply to go on with one's old work, but to do it henceforth from a motive of pure love. But, as a matter of fact, Brother Lawrence's own work in the convent kitchen was not his old work. He had been for many years a servant to a nobleman, and it was under a sense of Divine vocation that he entered a monastery as a lay brother, and was set to work in the kitchen. There is nothing in his life or teaching which supports the notion that sanctity consists in trying to "supernaturalize" work which is not our true vocation, and which we can leave if we choose. Its only legitimate application is either to work which is our vocation, or to work which we cannot escape.

But we have all but lost the sense of vocation. We often find ourselves in uncongenial employment, simply because we chose it in self-will at a time when it appeared congenial, and we were persuaded that we would always find it so. Or we remain in uncongenial employment into which we were thrust by circumstances, not because these circumstances continue to be insuperable, but because a change would mean financial loss and sheer hard toil for years to come.

Here is a youth, for instance, who was conscious of a call to be a doctor, but owing to inescapable circumstances, had to break off his studies and become a clerk. Today these circumstances are less unmanageable. He could, by dint of hard work and the most frugal of living, attain his first desire. But the prospect of giving up a steadily rising salary, and, in some cases even more, the sacrificing of comparatively ample leisure, or it may be the fear of being criticized and set down as "cranky" for starting at the bottom of the ladder when he was halfway up already and "going to school again," deters him from following his vocation.

It is not too much to say that two-thirds of those who plead uncongenial work as an excuse for their lack of spiritual joy and vigor, could change their employment tomorrow if they were willing to pay the price. Certain it is that Brother Lawrence did not have them in view when he declared that there was no work so mean and humdrum but that men could realize the presence of God in it. Still less sympathy would he have shown to those who imagine that they can practice the presence of God while engaged in dishonest, or even questionable, occupations, or indeed, in any occupation, however harmless in itself, about which their consciences are in doubt. The whole question of vocation is intimately connected with prayer; and many an aspiring soul finds prayer a weariness, if not a torture, simply because it lacks the courage to face the question as to whether its daily work is in a line with its true vocation. "The trivial round, the common task," will not in itself "furnish all we ought to ask." If mending shoes runs counter to God's will for us, it will prove as inimical to our spiritual life as the most ambitious self-chosen career. Self-will, or sheer spineless drifting with the tide, is every bit as wrong in homespun as in purple, and to remain in the kitchen from sheer laziness and cowardice is as reprehensible as to usurp the throne from motives of greed and ambition.

It all runs back into the question which lies at the root of the spiritual life: Is the central element in our communion with God an act of self-surrender, or is it, on the contrary, a demand of self-love? Is the symbol of our prayer the open hand, or the open heart? Are we using God as a means of self-realization, or are we offering ourselves as a means of glorifying Him? And if we mean self-surrender, has our offering been made in an honest, generous spirit, unconditionally and without reservations? Have we interpreted it emotionally, or are we seeking to work it out in the affairs of daily life? Upon our answer to these questions it will depend whether our spiritual life is a sectional, sophisticated business, an accentric new patch on an old garment, or the transmuting of the whole life into the life of God.

Our prayer life will be creative just in as far as our whole life is charged with the creative energy of God. We need not waste our time in asking for the Apostolic power in prayer until we have learned to say with the Apostle, "I live; yet not I, but Christ liveth in me." From beginning to end, it is the presuppositions behind prayer that we need to be chiefly concerned about. Let the *law* of prayer be observed, and its *method* can take care of itself. Our preoccupation with theories and ways of prayer is as superficial and essentially unintelligent as the superstitious insistence of certain revivalists upon "knee drill." There is only one thing indispensable—a soul willing to let go of self and to live henceforth in God. "The mark of a saint," Bishop Westcott reminds us, "is not perfection, but consecration. A saint is not a man without faults, but a man who has given himself without reserve to God." And, rightly understood, one act of self-surrender can make a saint. Here is our only true wisdom in prayer, and here the only method that is of universal application.

The Path to Power

It is a common experience among those who through the
gate of prayer have entered into newness of life that, after
the first rush of joyful wonder as the soul looks out upon
a world of unguessed beauty, a sense of disappointment
gathers and grows. It is not that we doubt the reality of
the life divinely imparted: it is that we are surprised at its
feebleness. In the first flush of joy we seemed to possess the
strength of those that wait upon the Lord. We mounted
up with wings as eagles; we ran all day long and were not
weary. With our surrender to God, power seemed to pour
into our soul; we seemed charged with creative potency;
the wonder that had been wrought within us seemed to
possess a magic, self-reproducing quality. For a brief space
we saw ourselves sharing the wonderful spiritual fecundity
of the great saints which enriched the Church again and
again with "new families." Wherever we went we found
spiritual friends; in every eye we seemed to meet a response
to our unspoken appeal.

But soon the glory faded. We could no longer fly or run;
we could not even walk without growing faint. Where
once there had been rivers of living water, there was now
but a faint trickle. Prayer, once so potently creative, could
barely sustain the new man it had brought into being.
Doubts as to the completeness of our surrender suggested

themselves, and far more destructive doubts as to the validity of the law of surrender. Were we not, after all, deceived by a religious catchword? Is not this doctrine of the yielded self as mechanical as any of the short cuts to salvation which are the stock in trade of itinerant evangelists? And if we were saved from capitulating to such doubt, it was only by the irrefutable fact that the little flame of life continued to burn within us—flickering, feeble, intermittent, but impossible to explain away. In the end we resigned ourselves to a mere spiritual existence. The flame, we argued, must remain dim and wind-blown in a world that is at war with God. Only exceptional souls need expect to be powerfully and influentially alive where everything conspires to crush and annihilate.

But such resignation, once we face issues squarely, is intolerable to an honest mind. To say that prayer which begins as a channel of creative power must continue and end as something that barely keeps us alive and no more, is to give away the whole case. If an act of devotion opened our soul's floodgates to the inrush of God's creative energy, shall a life of devotion do less? Must it not rather involve the cumulative force of a succession of such acts, and a succession so close as to make of all life a habit of surrender as continuous and inevitable as breathing? If our life is feeble and impotent, it can only be so from one of two causes: either we do not yet understand the law of surrender in its application to daily living, or, understanding it, we have failed to apply it. There is no room for a third alternative. God does not despise the weak—but He does not create weaklings.

Why, then, do we remain weak in spite of our devotion? One of the Fathers of the Desert once compared the love of praise to an onion. When stripped of one skin it is found to be sheathed in another, and as often as you strip it, you will find it still protected. The same might be said of self-love. It is not enough to put it to death once by a definite act of self-surrender; it must be put to death daily. Beneath each sheath of self-regard and vainglory there is another; and if we think that the soul can be stripped of it once and for all, we have still to learn the very elements of the spiritual life. There is no magic word of surrender that will annihilate self-seeking. One true act of surrender is sufficient to dethrone self, but the uncrowned king becomes the murderous conspirator; and nothing short of a life's discipline, a daily dying to self, not in pious imagination, but by a succession of stern, practical acts of self-denial, will rout the enemy. Until we have begun to understand this and to turn it into practice, we have not set foot upon the path to power.

I

Let a soul live with God, and it will hate everything that is mean and vile. Let it look on the beauty of God, and it too will become beautiful. Let it love God, and "the expulsive power of a new affection" will do what a lifetime of self-torture cannot do. St. Augustine well said, "Love, and do what you like."

That the soul that lives with God and lives in God and lives God will be transformed into that same image from glory to glory, is, of course, splendidly true; but, as a matter of hard fact, it is precisely that intimate transforming union with God that is for most of us impossible until, by steady self-discipline, we have cleared away the hindrances to such union. This does not mean that we must wait for union with God until all that hinders is cleared away by dint of laborious effort, but that we must in union with God mortify our members which are upon earth to the perfecting of that union. There are elect souls whose growth is as that of the lily, and they are of the *grand race;* but the majority of people who insist that the spiritual life must be of the lily order are unfortunately themselves far more like thistles than lilies. One cannot, for instance, take part in church life without being struck by the personal touchiness and ambition of many church workers; and in nearly every case the petty self-seeking that is the scandal of religious life is most accentuated, as, indeed, one would expect it to be, in those who most vehemently insist that the Christian life is not an affair of rule or method, but a free, spontaneous response to a spiritual environment—a response as natural as breathing. They seem pathetically unaware that their theory has so little worked in their own case that they have not even succeeded in eliminating self-interest in holy things, let alone in everyday life.

But we are still left with the objection that even if it be the case that self-discipline is an essential condition of true self-realization, and something in us has got to die before we can achieve fulness of life, it still remains true that the Christian's quarrel is with sin, and not with the innocent natural human impulse. For practical purposes it is impossible to separate sin, in cut and dried fashion, from the natural impulses through which it manifests itself, and into whose fiber it has insinuated itself. We cannot, for instance, say, "I will kill my ignoble deference to the opinion of men," without saying in the same breath, "I will mortify that perfectly natural and innocent love of approbation which is part of my makeup." We cannot fight against sins of the tongue without doing violence to that, in itself, quite harmless talkativeness which gives these sins a chance. We cannot master the lusts of the flesh without dealing sternly with the body which is their instrument. We cannot combat pride without humbling and chastening our natural self-esteem. No artificial distinction between fighting against sin and fortifying our natures will stand, once we get down to the bedrock of reality. There is none so spiritual, or so devoted to God's service, as not to need constant mortification, lest having preached to others, he himself become a castaway.

The way to life is, of necessity, a strait and narrow way, and there are many rough places and lonely valleys awaiting the pilgrim. But it is doubly hard (though we are slow to believe it) for him who has not learned the royal secret of mortification. Our habitual misuse of words has led us to imagine that Christian freedom consists in the liberty to follow the mood and impulse of the moment, and we protest against anything that would put fetters upon this liberty. Spontaneity, we say, spells joyousness, and joy is the very essence of Christianity. And yet, when we go below the surface, we cannot disguise from ourselves that our cult of spontaeity and freedom has brought us no increase of joy. Quite on the contrary, our religious life is pitched in the minor key, and our public worship, where it is not frigidly formal, is marked by wistfulness and pathos rather than by joyfulness.

True spontaneousness is the fruit of discipline. It is the artist who has mastered the technique of his art most perfectly, who can best respond to the vision and inspiration of the moment. How many painters have failed to express their vision, because the energy that ought to have gone to its recording was spent in a vain struggle with an imperfectly mastered medium? How many poets and writers lose their most sublime inspirations in their search for the luminous phrase, the revealing word? It is the same in the art of life. If we would single out one thing above any other that blights our spiritual life with sadness, it is our sheer futility. We perceive our vocation, but cannot bend our intelligence and our wills to our vision. A crisis calls us, but our moral and spiritual fiber is too slack to meet its stern demands. A stirring message thrills us with new joy and hope, but our vagrant moods quench the newfound light, and we pay for our golden moment with long, leaden hours of reaction. And if we deal faithfully with ourselves, we shall come to the conclusion that our futility is rooted in lawlessness and self-indulgence. During a period of war many a man who had lived comfortably and at ease and found life a dreary, ineffectual business, suddenly discovers a well of joy and power in himself, once he endures the hard discipline of camp and fighting line. And we may experience the same change in our spiritual life, if we would only discard our dilettante conception of freedom and go into the front lines with Christ.

There is among us an unhealthy cult of life which militates against the ideal of discipline. In our anxiety to lay due emphasis upon the positive, constructive character of Christianity, we have made a shibboleth of its doctrine of free, abundant, overflowing life, athrill with splendid vigor and indefeasible gladness. There is far too much talk about life and living to be healthy, far too much of deliberate and self-conscious cultivation of vitality to be safe. And as one watches certain perfervid apostles of life, one is not impressed by their own vital quality. So far from reproducing the strong, steady, triumphant life of their Master, their energy seems to exhaust itself in a somewhat flamboyant and hectic paraphrase of certain elements in His teaching. Only too often they exhibit a flabby, loafing, feverish habit which suggests a very low vitality indeed. There is nothing to be surprised at in this. Even in the spiritual realm —one had almost said, most of all in the spiritual realm— it holds good that he who seeketh his own life shall lose it. We must at all costs recover the splendid spiritual courage that casts life behind its back, that puts self beneath its feet. That royal habit of soul may conceivably be created and sustained without daily discipline and mortification; but if so, we have no record of such an achievement in all the annals of sanctity. One imagines that few would care to maintain that their own lives are the brilliant exception to this rule!

And if life is one key word of the present age, love is another. We claim to have discovered "the greatest thing in the world" as none of our forefathers did; to have gained an insight into the hidden beauties and delicacies of love which past generations lacked. We define our faith in terms of love, and reduce all mortality to love. But with all our newborn sensitiveness and delicacy of perception, our love lacks largeness and fixity. It is an emotion rather than a principle. It makes sympathetic, highly-strung personalities of us: it does not make us men who are as a hiding place from the wind and a covert from the tempest. It begets in us a restless passion for service: it does not breed an immutable sense of vocation. It quickens our imaginative insight into the lives of others: it does not lead us so to identify ourselves with the common life of our brethren that we share not so much their sorrows and failures, but the atoning sorrow and sacrifice of the common Savior.

Again the key to the problem is discipline. In the last resort, both love and life resolve themselves into *spiritual staying power*. And there is no spiritual staying power without lifelong, unrelenting discipline.

II

Try as we may, we cannot escape from the ascetic principle in Christian living—a principle, as someone has remarked, "as deeply seated in human nature as domesticity itself." This does not mean, of course, either that all asceticism is Christian, or that Christianity can be exhausted in terms of asceticism.

Christian asceticism is always distinguished by two guiding marks: *its motive is not a desire to acquire superior merit, or to achieve self-improvement, but an impulse of pure love; and it begins, not with the body, but with the spirit.*

It is by its motive that Christian asceticism is lifted out of the region of gloom and becomes a minister of gladness. The Christian soul longs to endure hardness, to toil, to suffer, to deny itself to the death, not for purposes of spiritual self-aggrandizement, but out of a consuming desire to share the labors and sufferings of Him who submitted Himself to the limitations and disciplines of a poor man's life for our sakes. It was the passion to be brought into fuller sympathy and closer union with the Man of Sorrows that made St. Teresa cry out, "Let me suffer, or not live!" *No mortification can be called fully Christian which is not an authentic, irrepressible movement of love.* And such mortification will leave its impress upon our prayer life. One act of self-denial with the master motive of love behind it can transform our praying from the beating of the empty air into the power that removes mountains. There is only one secret of prevailing prayer—the love that crucifies self, and enthrones God in a lifelong series of definite acts of love; and when we come to analyze these acts, we shall see that behind even the most spontaneous and positive of them is the practice of daily mortification.

This mortification has nothing in common with self torture. Its aim is not the mutilation of suppression, let alone the extinction, of the natural powers, but their right use in the service of love. It makes not for death, but for life. Its spirit is positive and constructive. If, for instance, we mortify our tongue, it is not that we may reduce it to silence, but that we may fit it to speak good tidings of great joy. Suddenly—after months of severe restraint, perhaps—we find ourselves able to speak words that make dull eyes to shine and hard hearts to yield. We know now why we had to keep silent so long. Before we put the bridle on our tongues, our words were idle and impotent; now they are charged with vital power. And the keeping of silence and the going forth into speech are twin movements of the same love. It was the love that burns to fit ourselves for the Master's use that prompted the silence; it was the love that yields all faculties to God that He might use them that inspired the utterance. And love is pure joy. Christian mortification is not a dreary penance. Its restraints are radiant with promise and hope; its austerities are the luxuries of the heart that loves. The truly self-disciplined soul has all the attractiveness of one who is ruled by love. Self-regarding asceticism develops the stronger but less lovely traits of a man's character: Christian mortification is a soil in which sweetness and natural virtues spring up like flowers. As we have said already, the Christian ascetic has always attracted men by his sheer gaiety of heart.

It is the motive of Christian asceticism which confers authority upon it. We cannot read the life of our Lord with unprejudiced vision without realizing that He trod the path of daily self-denial, in small things as well as great, that indeed "His life is our way." When we remember that He once fasted for forty days, and often spent long, cold nights in prayer, we are only touching the outermost fringe of His devotion. When we realize that He endured insults and bitter scorn in perfect meekness, we are only laying our finger on certain striking symptoms of a deep-rooted habit. It is as we study His methods as a teacher, His bearing as a healer, His conduct as a friend, His wisdom as a leader, His skill as a seeker of the lost that we gain any degree of insight into the depth and completeness of His self-abnegation, His unreserved self-surrender, His Divine humility. "Measure all by the Cross," says Robertson of Brighton. "Do you want success? The Cross was failure. Do you want a name? The Cross is infamy. Is it to be gay and happy that you live? The Cross is pain and sharpness. Do you live that the will of God may be done in you and by you in life and death? Then, and only then, the spirit of the Cross is in you. When once a man has learned that, the power of the world is gone; and no man need bid him, in denunciation or in invitation, not to love the world." Jesus lived supremely in the spirit of the Cross, and it is the Cross—not merely the historic Cross upon Calvary, but the Cross in the heart of God, the principle of sacrifice which lies at the foundation of the universe—which gives its justification and its power to Christian asceticism. We sometimes forget that the way of the Cross is not only the way of the Savior to the soul of man, and the ultimate path of the cosmos itself to its destiny: it is also the soul's way to God; and to let Jesus bear the Cross alone is the most deadly way of making that Cross of none effect.

We are now in the position to see the bearing of self-discipline and mortification upon prayer. Mortification, in so far as it is truly Christian, is nothing else than "the practice of the Cross." The spirit of the Cross is the soul of true prayer; for, as we have seen, prayer is fundamentally an act of self-giving. We cannot really know the nature and the power of prayer until we know something of what it means to be crucified with Christ. The soul that is not united to the Crucified cannot give itself in prayer. Prayer that has a vital background and is a fit channel of power is always a hard and humiliating business. Its strength resides, not in its freedom, but in its limitations; not in its exuberance, but in its restraints. We sometimes plead that we are temperamentally unfitted for the life of prayer; and it may well be that our natural disposition and make up are incompatible with one type of devotion or another. But the prayer which we have defined as creative is not a matter of temperament at all. What hinders us from achieving it is simply our share in the common human disinclination to face reality, and in the common human fear of the cross. Once we are willing to take up the cross and follow Jesus, we have already begun to pray.

Romantic heroism would cry, "Lo, I have come to save the world by the bitter death of the Cross." Divine obedience said, "Lo, I come to do Thy will, O God."

III

That most scantily appreciated of all the Collects in the Anglican Prayer Book—the Collect for the Feast of the Circumcision—might well serve as the motto of those who desire to find the true path to power. "Grant us the true circumcision of the spirit, that our hearts and all our members being mortified from all wordly and carnal lusts, we may in all things obey thy blessed will."

With all our polemic against externalism in religion and our emphasis upon its spiritual character, we are very slow to learn that the strategic center of our spiritual warfare is not the body with its appetites, or the mind with its ambitions, but the spirit itself. That is why our progress in the Christian life is often so disappointing. We offer ourselves to God, renouncing material self-indulgence and wordly ambition. We keep a watchful eye over our physical and mental activities, striving to yield all our members as instruments of righteousness. And yet we fail. Our lives are reformed, but, on the whole, impotent. Our Christianity is undoubtedly there, but it does not shine, does not radiate. Our prayers comfort us in trouble and support us in our struggle, but they lack dynamic. They do not create new situations; they do not even transform old situations, but only make them tolerable. Presently we find ourselves suffering from spiritual lassitude and ennui. We groan under a weariness that is worse than failure. It is not that our spiritual life does not work, but that it works as indifferently as our smoke laden lungs, our ill-organized business, our wobbly political machine, our haphazard system of education. It is not the miracle of and glory of our life; it is only one of its many mediocrities.

There is only one cure—to begin at the center. We have sought to mortify our worldly ambition: what about our spiritual ambition? We have tried to regulate our domestic emotions: what about our religious emotions? One sometimes hears religious people lamenting the defections and failures of the Church, and then adding, by way of consolation: "But there is so much genuine goodness, so much unconscious Christianity among people outside the Churches, that really we need not be unduly depressed about the religious situation." But that is to take an entirely superficial view of the matter. If there is a vast amount of unrecognized and often unconscious Christianity today, it is ultimately derived, if not from the organized Churches (a matter which is open to discussion), most assuredly from that which the Churches have produced and conserved throughout the centuries.

It is from the society of the redeemed that redemptive influences radiate; it is through His body, however sorely wounded and maimed, that Christ is seeking to manifest Himself to the world. And if that body be indeed sick unto death, the world must ultimately suffer a loss that is all the more tragic the less it is recognized. If the House of God becomes a den of thieves, what can we expect from the city; if the priest profanes the altar, what hope is there for the people? The work of purging must begin in the sanctuary. We need not fear that the world will be left in darkness, so long as the altar lights are kept burning.

This is unpopular doctrine, but it holds the key to life. The first step on the path to power, whether for Churches or for individuals, is to expel the traffic of spiritual ambition and religious success mongering, and to guard the religious emotions with unceasing vigilance. If one were asked to single out the one weakness which, more than any other, has robbed both individual and corporate Christian life of power, one would say it is that unwillingness to endure rigorous self-denial which is so characteristic of our age. In the individual the lack of discipline most often takes the shape of an unbridled surrender to the religious mood or emotion of the moment an unquestioning gratification of personal affinities, tastes and ambitions. In corporate life this spirit of self-seeking expresses itself often in sensuous ritual without the safeguard of lofty doctrine or wholesome moral discipline, in a sensational revivalism which panders to the crude emotions, or an ambitious intellectualism which flatters the dilettante understanding, but leaves the spiritual nature of man untouched. Our private devotions and our public worship are alike shorn of power for lack of that stern and persistent discipline which is its natural background. It is as useless to expect creative prayer and dynamic worship to spring from an undisciplined habit of life which yields to every impulse and puts self-expression in the forefront, as it is to expect to gather grapes from thistles. Let us face the fact that we are at war with the forces of unbelief and sin, and that the first requisite for war is a trained soldiery. No amount of glowing emotion, flashing insight, and eagerness for action can make up for the lack of that iron in the soul that comes from enduring the hardness of the Christian soldier. In our churches are many well-meaning people, some of them exceedingly attractive in their eagerness to do good and their quick appreciation of everything high and lovely, who have never learned to say No to their natural impulses and inclinations

—especially when these impulses and inclinations operate in the realm of religion—and who have never troubled to question their affinities or to sift their motives. And the result is that powerlessness which is the problem, and the reproach of the Church of Christ today.

IV

The question of bodily discipline should normally arise out of the question of spiritual discipline, and considered in its relation to the spiritual, it is not likely to betray us into sterile excesses. Two familiar truisms emerge at the very outset. On the one hand, bodily discipline cannot be ignored because body and spirit are inextricably intertwined; and, on the other hand, it should always be kept in a strictly subordinate place. On the first point little needs to be said. The days when people looked upon the soul as an entity entirely independent of the body, which, for all spiritual purposes, might be conceived of as functioning a million miles away from the body, are past. Philosophy knows nothing of such an entity; and laboratory psychology has driven home the humiliating truth that a good dinner may transport the soul from spiritual wistfulness to gross complacency, and a grain of an Eastern drug exalt it to the realm of ecstatic vision, or plunge it into the gloom of the vilest hells. We cannot any longer preach a gospel of the spirit which ignores the body, but while we rightly emphasize the need for a redemption which includes the ill-housed, starved, stunted body of the slum dweller as well as his soul, we are not so quick to insist that the man who fails to discipline his body, let alone the man who pampers it, need not hope to achieve spiritual strength and beauty.

No man who neglects bodily discipline—whether he be a well paid artisan gorging himself with coarse food, or an aristocrat of culture choosing his refined physical pleasures with artistic restraint—can enter the kingdom which God has prepared for him. Discipline is not merely a matter of refraining from excess. As in the things of the spirit, so in the things of the body, Christian discipline means the uprooting of self-gratification and self-will. The refined man who elects to have simple meals and simple clothing, but who chooses each course and each garment with no other thought than his own health, taste, and predilections, is as undisciplined, and as really given over to the flesh, as the gourmand and the luxuriously arrayed.

Here is the crux of the matter. We believe in physical mortification, not because we esteem the body as vile, but, on the contrary, because our faith in the Incarnation pledges us to a high conception of the body's sanctity and destiny. Mortification is not the sacrificing of the body to the alleged interests of the soul: it is the expression of the soul's regard for the body as an instrument of holiness. The body is meant to be not the mere outer garmenting, but the palpitant medium of the soul—to take on its mould, and to glow with its splendor. It is destined itself to become spiritual, not by means of a process of inanition, as a false asceticism would have us believe, but by a gradual transfiguration in which no natural endowment is lost. It is possible for a man to become radiantly and triumphantly Christian under the most hostile circumstances, and in the most degrading environment. But it is *not* possible for a man to enter upon his full Christian birthright without severe discipline of body as well as of spirit. A man's environment may be ideal, and every circumstance conspire to further his highest development, but if he imagines that he can achieve his spiritual destiny with a slack fibered, capricious, pampered body, he is laboring under a tragic delusion. More spiritual failure—especially failure in prayer —than we like to think, can be traced to bodily slackness.

So far from being wrong, it is a matter of sheer common sense that a man whose circumstances afford no opportunities for enduring the hardness of the Christian soldier should seek such opportunities for himself, provided always they be sought along sane lines, involving no neglect of common duty, and chosen in humble dependence upon the leading of God, who works through man's choice as well as through circumstances.

V

Those who have set themselves whole-heartedly upon the path that leads from self to God, will sooner or later be confronted with the demand for renunciation. The demand may come in the line of everyday activity, leaving us free to follow our accustomed mode of living, but with a new spirit of self-abnegation; or it may come, as it did to St. Francis, as a call to renounce things wholly lawful in themselves and to follow Christ in the way of literal poverty and self-stripping—"naked to follow the naked Jesus," to use the bald phrase of *The Imitation*. It has been the habit of Protestant piety to deny the validity of these particular and purely individual vocations, and to insist upon one way of discipleship for all. But Christ Himself sanctioned such special vocations, and enjoined upon those who did not have them to put no hindrance in the way of their brethren who felt themselves called in such ways. "He that is able to receive it, let him receive it," was our Lord's ruling regarding such as "made themselves eunuchs for the Kingdom of Heaven's sake."

The world is waiting for souls who are wholly detached from earthly considerations and wholly attached to God. It is for want of complete detachment—the necessary condition of whole-hearted attachment—that our faith remains dim and our prayer feeble. It was a common saying among the Fathers of the Desert that if a man took more thought for his life than was necessary to keep him alive, he was not fit for the highest type of prayer, and we are now discovering how right their instinct was. Looking back over the curious inefficiency of so much in recent religious effort, which was born of a genuine vision but lacked staying-power; looking back also upon one's personal prayer life, which mirrors the age in so many ways, one realizes as never before that the first foundation of any valid spiritual work is *a detached heart*. Nothing can make up for the lack of a disentangled heart; spiritual vision and insight, moral earnestness, religious genius are futile, so long as the heart remains attached to earthly comforts and allurements. We long to recall a Christless world and a weakened Church to eternal values, to persuade Christian souls especially to turn from the temptations of mammon and the tyranny of false social standards and unchristian distinctions, and to realize their brotherhood in Christ and their citizenship in the Kingdom of God. But who is sufficient for these things?

Might it not be that at the root of our weakness in prayer and of our lurking doubt as to the efficacy of prayer, there lies this unanswered call, this unobeyed vision? Is it not possible that the disquieting spiritual ebb-tide of today is due to the fact that many of us have refused a call to take the way of the Incarnation? Certain it is that if we would be spiritually powerful, we must take our Lord's path to power.

Jesus on one occasion, seeing the multitude following Him, turned, not to His disciples as at other times, but to the motley crowd of common folk, and said: "If any man come to me, and hate not his father, and mother, and wife, and children, and brethren, and sisters, yea, and his own life also, he cannot be My disciple. And whosoever doth not bear his cross, and come after me, cannot be my disciple. . . . Whosoever he be of you that forsaketh not all that he hath, he cannot be my disciple." And still that call comes to every man, and remains the inexorable condition of discipleship.

6

The Apostolate of Prayer

There is no aspect of the prayer life round which controversy has spun so baffling a web as intercession. How can prayer benefit anyone beyond the person who prays? How can prayer on behalf of others be effectual without infringing upon their free will? Why should the sick person who happens to have praying friends stand a better chance of recovery than the equally deserving sick person who has no one to say a prayer on his behalf? If prayer admittedly cannot change natural law, why should we expect it to change the laws which govern the moral and intellectual nature of those we pray for? These and a host of other much debated questions have wrapped the subject in an obscuring cloud of controversial dust, and not a few of the answers given by orthodox apologists for prayer serve only to render that cloud more dense.

Whereas in former times intercession was looked upon as hard toil for strong men, it has come to be regarded by the majority of people as a nice, quiet occupation especially suitable for delicate persons and invalids. Comparatively few look upon it as part of a Christian man's vocation.

As a matter of fact, we still tend to interpret prayer apart from its larger context, in spite of the undeniable gains which the modern attitude has brought us. Intercessory prayer cannot be interpreted *in vacuo;* it presupposes a spiritual universe, a world of grace within which alone it finds its justification. So long as we interpret the world and man's destiny merely in terms of science and philosophy, our faith in intercessory prayer must of necessity be at the mercy of the latest scientific or philosophical theory. But if we enter the world of grace—a world redeemed, recreated, and unified in Christ—intercession becomes the most convincing and luminous fact in the world, and every valid result of scientific and philosophical enquiry will ultimately contribute to its right interpretation.

We have seen that prayer is based upon the conception of God as fullness of love. Every real prayer is the soul's response to that love in an act of self-surrender. The life of prayer is the life of conversion—a gradual, progressive turning from self to God. Potentially and ideally, that conversion is accomplished in the first genuine act of surrender, whereby the soul dissociates itself from sin and enters into its right relation with Eternal Love; actually it involves a lifetime of successive and growingly complete acts of daily self-denial and daily integration into Christ, a yielding up of the self that it may be filled with the fullness of God, a losing of life that it may be found again in Him.

But this passing from the life of the flesh to the life that is hid with Christ in God is no mere pious sentiment or vague mysticism. It means the identification of the whole personality—mind, will, and emotion with the mind and will and heart of God. It means making Christ's interests our own. It means to learn to think with God: to have the mind of Christ, to see the world through His eyes, to share His passion to save and redeem. It has well been said that "the heart of Christ in the heart of the Christian is the vital center of practical Christianty, the living fountain of all its healing agencies." And that heart is formed in us by prayer.

I

It is at this point that the soul is drawn to the prayer of intercession. Prayer is seen as an apostolate—a means of making God known to others. We do not ask how our praying can influence other lives; we do not begin to wonder if preaching and teaching or acts of beneficence, are not far more rational and effective means of doing good in the world than prayer. These arguments have weight only with the man who approaches prayer theoretically, or who still regards it as merely a means of obtaining things from God where other means fail. But we know what prayer has wrought in our lives. We know that it has been effectual in as far as it has centered in an act of self-committal to God, and in a resolve to take up the Cross and follow Jesus in His self-sacrificing love. And we feel that since Christ Himself wrought out salvation for others by a life of obedience even to the death of the Cross, so we, being joined to Him and living in union with Him, can offer our prayers, and the life behind our prayers, on behalf of others.

Once we grasp the true nature of prayer, the difficulties which are so often urged against the practice of intercession are seen to be entirely irrelevant. Knowing all human life to be one; knowing ourselves to be vitally and indissolubly knit to our brethren in God; knowing that He sees mankind as living in relations of mutual interdependence, united by their common response to Eternal Love, intercession becomes a vital necessity. We see our mutual interdependence broken, because of the failure of so many to respond to the love of

God and take their place in His family; and the love of Christ constrains us to take His way of reaching these estranged ones.

Now we are in the position to realize how utterly mistaken that view of intercession is which relegates it to the weak and inactive. When Christ saw the fields of the world white unto harvest, He said, not to a group of dreamy mystics or holy invalids, but to the twelve sturdy men who were to carry His Gospel to the ends of the earth: "Pray ye therefore the Lord of the harvest, that he would send forth laborers into his harvest." Before the commission to preach and teach comes the vocation to prayer. It is at once the preliminary testing and the final triumph of the true apostle. It not only accompanies apostleship from beginning to end: it is itself an apostleship. The instinct of the Church was right when it recognized intercession as a distinct vocation, demanding all a strong man's powers, giving scope to his whole personality, sufficing as a life work for some of the noblest spirits and the brightest intellects. Our present day utilitarianism has driven that instinct underground; but it can never die. And the time is at hand when it will emerge once more, and elect souls in all the Churches will feel themselves called to a life of intercession. But while such a call necessarily comes to the few, all are meant to share in the apostolate of prayer. We need only glance through the Pauline Epistles to realize how large a part intercession played in the strenuous life of the itinerant Apostle. Of our Lord Himself it is recorded that He was so hard pressed with external activity that He had no leisure so much as to eat, yet He spent whole nights in prayer. No amount of activity can excuse us from the duty of intercession, and any activity, however spiritual it may seem, which incapacitates us for intercession is to be viewed with grave suspicion.

One reason why the man who looks at prayer from the outside tends to exalt preaching and practical philanthropy above intercession, is that he looks upon intercession from the point of view of those for whom it is offered. His sole object being to alleviate the sufferings and increase the happiness of those about whom he is anxious, the thought naturally occurs to him that an inspiring message, or a deed of kindly help, is by far the quicker and better way to reach them than "mere" prayer. After all, intercession is the expression of sympathy, and the same sympathy may find more effectual expression in other directions. But the true apostle of prayer has an entirely different point of departure. He starts not from his sense of the world's need, however poignant that sense may be, but from his realization of the deeper sorrow, the more intense longing, in the heart of Him who bids him to pray. The righting of His wrongs, the slaking of His thirst for the souls of men, the fulfilling of His desire that His disciples should watch with Him through the world's dark hour—these, and not merely his own necessarily fluctuating compassion for the sorrows and wrongs of man, drive him to prayer. Man's pain and wrong are acutely felt by him, but they reach him through the heart of Christ. So closely is he identified with Christ that no sword can pierce His heart without passing through his own also. Moreover, he has so truly entered into his Lord's worldwide longing that nothing short of intercession which embraces the whole world can content him. He has learned to think universally, not because he has reasoned himself out of insularity, but because his whole being is devoted to the Savior of the world, in whom all are made one.

And, as in personal prayer, the core of intercession is not

"asking things" for others, but an offering of one's soul to God that it may become a fit vehicle of His redeeming power. "O Thou Divine Lover of souls," cries the apostle of prayer, "make of me a true repairer of Thy wrongs, a true channel of Thy grace. Let no selfish interest dull me to anything that concerns Thy honor. Give me an apostolic heart, world-wide in its love for men—yea, let Thy love towards men be my very pulse!" The motto of the true intercessor must ever be: "For their sakes I sanctify myself."

It is as we trace the beginnings of apostolic intercession that we shall best be able to grasp its nature and scope. As we have already seen, prayer, in most cases, begins with personal petition. We ask benefits for ourselves and for those we love. Then we come to realize that the power of prayer lies not in the external benefit, or even in the mental and spiritual reinforcement, that comes to us through it, but in our communion with God. A new love takes possession of us, a new relationship transfigures life, a new world dawns upon our unsealed eyes. We know that communion with God does not only mean mastery over life, but that it is life itself. And as we humbly press closer to the heart of God and read a little of its secret, it is gradually borne in upon us that it is only as we die to self-love that we shall be able to take our true place within that heart of love. We see that prayer is a long and arduous pilgrimage from self to God; not, indeed, the pilgrimage of those who imagine that God can be reached by human effort, but the progress of souls that have been redeemed by Christ, and now desire to be wholly found in Him.

II

Very early in that pilgrimage we begin to include others, not near and dear to us, in our prayers; and that not from purely altruistic motives. We realize that our progress towards God depends very largely upon our fellows. We have friends who praise and indulge us, and sooner or later we recognize that their blind love is not helping us towards spiritual manhood. We also have detractors and enemies who work us ill, and we find ourselves again and again overcome of their evil, instead of being able to overcome it with good. We bring friend and foe into the circle of our prayer, and as we do this in any genuine sense, we find that the mere fact of bringing them into the presence of God changes their relation to us and ours to them. They are no longer merely human units to whose stimulus, whether for good or ill, we, as other human units, react. They are real or potential fellow citizens in the Kingdom of God, called by God to co-operate with Him and with us in the work of redemption. We see them more and more as the object of God's solicitude. He is seeking to guide and mould them; and it is their resistance to *Him* that is the most important factor in anything that may be wrong in their conduct towards us.

To lift them thus into the light of God changes our attitude towards them! and that not only by way of making us more patient and forgiving. It means that henceforth these friends and foes of ours will not find us as open to their influence as we were before. Praise will no longer unbalance our foolish minds; blame and injury will no longer sting us to weak self-defence and retaliation. Henceforth we see them in relation to God. There are no longer two but three in our thought of them—ourselves, they, and God. As we view them in Him, their power to annoy or weaken us is seen to be controlled and modified by the over-ruling power of Love. We realize that in the hands of that Love both the misguided kindness of friends and the malicious opposition of foes may be turned into so many means of grace and opportunities of progress. It is part of the mystery of that Divine alchemy by which Jesus Himself turned the dross of man's false friendship and malignant enmity into the pure gold of perfect Manhood and Saviorhood. In that miraculous transmutation we are called to co-operate, and intercession is the philosopher's stone which turns the clay of human perversity into material for the perfecting, not only of ourselves, but of the whole family of God. We learn to make capital of friend and foe alike; not, indeed, in using them as pawns in our game, but in so using their attitude and action towards us as to make them factors in our common redemption.

It is in the course of this extension of our prayer life to include those whose conduct seems to be a hindrance that we are, as a rule, first inspired with something of apostolic fervor. Through refusing to see either friend or foe out of his true relation to God, we realize our mutual dependence and indissoluble brotherhood in Him. And with that growing realization, and the closer communion with God which it involves, we catch something of the Divine sorrow for those of our brethren who have taken the wrong road. Sometimes in a flash, sometimes gradually, we are touched with something of God's own passion to redeem. Whether by preaching and teaching, by lowly deeds of kindness, or in the ways of social influence and homely friendship, we seek to recall men to their true center, to win them from the world and mammon and self to God.

But we soon find that our good is not strong enough to overcome the evil around us. We meet with misunderstanding and opposition, and our love is too feeble to remain patient and sweet. The warmth kindled by our apostolic zeal cannot survive the impact of man's coldness and disdain; we find it impossible not to dislike those who seem bent upon making themselves disagreeable. Or, if our love does not succumb to our natural distaste, it surrenders to our craze for popularity. We trim our message, and modify our counsel, and deflect our actions for the sake of winning favor, instead of enduring unpopularity that we may win souls. Or, again, we are tempted to secure a cheap emotional effect, to be content with surface impressions, to suppress troublesome points and evade difficult issues. If we are sufficiently honest to face facts, we gradually realize that, so far from our winning those to whom we are sent, they have mastered us. Almost imperceptibly we have come to regard them from a purely personal point of view, and not in their relation to God and His Kingdom. Their treatment of us has become the most important thing in our eyes, and where that treatment has been harsh, we see ourselves in the center of the picture as martyrs and heroes. Gradually the sense of our "wrongs" grows upon us, and our happiness comes to depend more and more upon the way in which people receive us.

There comes a moment when we realize that our work for God is a shoddy, futile business, unless it is backed at every point by the apostolate of prayer. We set out full of love, as we thought, and now we find it hard even to tolerate the men who oppose us. We thought our apostolic zeal would kindle a fire wherever we went, and now we need all our energy to keep its solitary embers from dying. Our wisdom lies in seeking to understand more deeply and share more fully our Lord's view of those who antagonize and distress us. What do they look like if seen against the background of the Cross? How does Christ regard them? It is only as we approach men from His side, and with His mind concerning them, that our view can be described as apostolic. We must represent not our own view, but the mind of Him who sent us; and we can only represent it truly as we become genuinely identified with it "from the inside," as it were, through sustained communion with Christ in His redeeming purpose. It is not a case of bearing with men "for Christ's sake," as conventional religion has it, but of looking at men through Christ's eyes, and seeing in them what He sees in them.

In one of those vivid and, to our modern sense, unpalatably realistic visions of St. Gertrude, we find our Lord showing His wounded arm wrenched and tortured on the Cross, and saying that whenever she prayed from her heart for certain malicious men who had wrought the monastery grievous harm, His arm was being restored. "But, Lord," cried St. Gertrude in amazement, "how canst Thou call such men Thine arm?" Comes the answer: "I call them so in truth, because they are members of the Body of which I glory to be the Head. Therefore the state of their souls causes me intense anxiety." Here is a picture, all the more telling because of its naïve mediæval crudeness, of the Christian conception of human solidarity. The image is worth pondering. If we could really believe that the men who oppose us at every point and make our ministry bitter for us are to Christ as a bruised and dislocated arm is to a man, how it would change our whole outlook! And it is "an image of the true." Our foes are not so much alien material that we must somehow transform into stones fit for the temple of God; they are members of the Body to which we belong—crippled and bruised members whose wounds cry for healing. Their sad condition is a challenge to the reality of our own membership in Christ's Body. Without them we cannot be made perfect; without them Christ Himself cannot perfect His work of restoration.

III

What is our real motive, our fundamental attitude, in seeking to win men? The true apostle goes forth dominated by the sense of His membership with all men in the Body of Christ, and by His consciousness of being sent to heal the wounds in the body of humanity, and the even more tragic wounds in the body of the Church. He thinks more of the Body than of the repulsive aspect of the sick members. He is animated by the vision of that Body healed and glorious, and not by any lesser triumph, whether of numbers or influence, or any of the other false allurements that beguile the Christian worker.

This may seem high mystical doctrine, but it has a most practical import. It faces us with the question as to whether, with all our religious experience and all our strenuous efforts, we are really doing very much to hasten the Kingdom for which Christ lived and died. That Kingdom, as we all admit, is of the spirit. In its upbuilding the motive and attitude of the builder count for everything. A coarse, selfish soul may build a very fine house; but where the House not made with hands is concerned, the man is the work. If, then, in our work among our fellows, we think much of the slights offered to us, or of the honor accorded to us; if our failures and successes loom large on our horizon; if we attach much importance to the type of person we influence, or to the effect our testimony has upon those we specially admire, we may be builders with God, but it is very doubtful if much of our work will survive the final test. The builder of the Kingdom must have his eye set on the Kingdom, his heart stayed on the King. He must think in terms of the Body. He must bear Himself as a member speaking and acting out of the consciousness of that membership, caring little for his own small achievements and reverses, and caring everything for the Body of Christ.

No one will pretend that this attitude is natural to us, or that it is easily acquired. It is entirely a product of apostolic prayer, and apostolic prayer is no light undertaking. To beseech blessings for others is comparatively easy, though genuine prayer of any kind is not accomplished without some sweat of soul. But so to offer ourselves to God as to renounce our own thoughts and feelings about our fellows and to accept His instead, brooding upon them until they become inwoven into our very fiber—that is indeed a task demanding the most heroic qualities. And to this task even the weakest are called, in their own measure. To every Christian soul the Divine Council Chamber is thrown open. God takes us into His confidence. He wants us to understand and have a share in His decrees of love. He wants apostles, ambassadors who really know His mind, consecrated souls so intimately united to Him that they can deal with any situation in His name and in His spirit.

And this opens up a new depth in prayer. If we are to know God's mind, and to know it so intimately as to be able actually to represent it, in our poor human measure, then prayer must involve not merely the outpouring of our souls to God, but also the outpouring of God's heart to us. This seems too startlingly big to be true, but nothing less can equip us for our apostolate. God wants to find a voice, as it were, in the world. He longs to express Himself to men. He calls for channels of expression—Christian souls who will continue the work of the Incarnation, and be to Him as his tongue is to a man. It is free personalities that He desires. He calls for living intelligences, for free agents, who shall interpret Him out of the abundance of their rich human nature, and under no domination or control save that of love. God's apostles are not passive channels, but active interpreters and exponents of a love which has become their very being. But this implies a reciprocity in prayer. God, as well as man, must become vocal. There can be no free appropriation of the Divine standpoint, unless God Himself explains His longings and opens His heart to the surrendered soul. That He actually does this is a matter of experience. As we become naturalized in the world of prayer, bringing our intellect, as well as our will, to bear upon our communion with God, making our reading and thinking, as well as our daily life, minister to its perfecting, we become conscious of what the mystics have called the "in-speaking" of God in the depth of the soul. Gently but surely, God reveals Himself. Old things gain a new aspect; the world of men is seen in a new light. We know ourselves, and we know God, as we have never done before. Facts of faith become more real and unassailable than facts of sense.

We have, as it were, entered the open heart of God, and are being transformed into its likeness, not by any magic of the religious imagination, but by the sure process of inter-communion.

And gradually we become conscious that as we abide in this state of intercommunion in wholehearted, humble self-surrender, our prayers will be inspired by His overshadowing spirit. Without any loss of freedom, we shall hear the Lord "pray His prayer within us," and know that the Spirit Himself maketh intercession for us. A new sense of calm confidence, a new assurance of victory, will possess us. In the final expression of self-surrender, we shall know our wills—no longer perverse and mistaken, but functioning harmoniously within the will of God. Not bowed in sad submission, but lifted up in humble gladness to the great and glorious Will of God, our wills shall share in the life of apostolic prayer. "Father, I *will*"—it is the will yoked to sacrificial love that speaks. And this wondrous alchemy which transmutes the dross of self-will into the royal gold of God's will become ours is wrought in the secret workshop of the soul.

IV

To have the will of God, the mind of Christ, concerning ourselves and the world, and to have them not merely by way of intellectual assent or moral appreciation, but by a vital appropriation that assimilates us to our Lord, is to have the key to apostolic power. Apart from such assimilation, we constantly relapse into a pessimistic view of the prospects of the Kingdom of God upon earth. We see evil triumphant and goodness mocked. We are chilled and disheartened by the mediocrity and feebleness of the good, the compromising weakness of religious men, and the dishonoring timidity of the Churches. We see prophets crying in the wilderness, preachers preaching to empty pews, evangelists trying in vain to make the appeal of the Gospel more attractive than the appeal of mammon and pleasure. There seems to be a plethora of institutions and works and an appalling amount of money spent to comparatively little effect. We think we could do with half the churches we have, and more than half of our workers might be better occupied in attending evening classes and working at their own improvement. And so we adduce a formidable volume of evidence to prove that things are in a bad way, and that the Church of Christ is dying.

But when we turn from our own interpretation of facts to Christ's vision of the world, we find ourselves breathing in another atmosphere. We said, in effect: "The harvest truly is small, and the laborers all too many; that is why they quarrel and wrangle with each other over a handful of ears." Jesus says: "The harvest truly is great, but the laborers are few"; that is why the barns remain empty. It is our vision that is at fault. No one can reap a harvest he does not see. We look for our harvest in the people who attend our churches, the money that is contributed to religious objects, the prestige and honor enjoyed by organized religious bodies and their leaders. But Christ looks out upon the world of men. They are His harvest, waiting to be reaped; in them He sees riches enough to fill the treasury of heaven to overflowing. If the Church of Christ gave herself to prayer, bent on discovering the mind of her Lord, thirsting to be transformed to His will and purpose, she would surely be led into fields white unto harvest.

But such prayer would make short work of many of our most cherished theories and methods. Matters about which we are almost feverishly concerned would appear as harmless, but quite unimportant side-issues; modes of work and habits of corporate life to which we are wedded would have to go as so much hampering lumber. We would realize that recognition by the world matters very little; that the only influence that counts is the influence we have in the secret place of prayer. As the Church appears before God, so she really is. If her influence there is negligible, then whatever influence she may seem to wield in the world is so much froth and moonshine. The true life of the Church, as of the individual, is hid with Christ in God. There are times when that life manifests itself in attracting the masses, as it did in the great historical Revivals; but some of the sublimest triumphs of Christ in the world are hidden—hidden often most of all from the workers themselves—and He who is meek and lowly in heart glories in these unseen conquests. Unless, therefore, both the Church and the Christian soul are prepared to accept Christ's vision, and seek first of all and most of all the life and strength that are hidden from the eyes of the world, true success is impossible, and we must content ourselves with a newspaper triumph.

In apostolic prayer lies the Churches' only hope of renewal. Once we learn to pray, individually and corporately, as Christ meant His messengers to pray, the nightmare of an unready world in which preachers and workers have to struggle for spiritual existence will dissolve in the light of day. Instead we see a world of men waiting—listening for the footfall of him who preaches the Gospel of peace. Men will not come into our churches, we lament. But they will come into the House of God not made with hands. By what authority were we told to measure the triumph of the Spirit by the number of buildings we can fill? We have the truth of God; we have the good news from God; we have the Living Christ. And the world is full of souls who are waiting for what we have to give; it is a matter of going out into the highways and giving our witness bravely and simply. We need not assume the attitude of shrewd dialecticians, adroit apologists, fervent and feverish persuaders and advocates. Christ has already spoken His almighty word in the depth of each soul; before the worker knew his vocation, the Spirit has been at work in the hearts of those to whom he is sent. The Lord always goes before His apostles, and [their] best ally is the unseen Witness in the human heart. It is our faithless habit of substituting argument for witness and criticism for affirmation that makes so much of our activity futile. It is our obsession with buildings and institutions that paralyzes us at the critical juncture. Once we grasp it firmly that we need not trouble about maintaining anything made of bricks and mortar, that the only thing we have to do is to bring Christ to men, we shall be quit of our misgivings and despondency.

This does not mean belittling the Church. On the contrary, it were well if we pondered the old saying, "Outside the Church, no salvation." There *is* a Church outside which there is no salvation—the living Body of Christ. Where that Body is healthy, such matters as buildings and maintenance, the status of the ministry, and the organization of its propaganda have a way of taking care of themselves.

The more strongly we believe in the Divine origin and function of the Church, the less we will worry about organization and finance. The Church, to take the most moderate view, is not only the corporate witness to Christ's presence among men, but the organ, as it were, of that presence; and this means that the one thing we need concern ourselves about is *that the Church shall really be a Church*—Holy, Catholic, and Apostolic; a witness and an organ of Christ on earth, and not a coterie of those who happen to share the same opinions and inherit the same prejudices. Our anxiety about the institutional aspect of Church life and work has its root in a lurking doubt as to the Divine authority behind the Church. We are not quite sure if the Church is not only one among many religious institutions destined to serve their purpose and then disappear. There is but one way of proving the Apostolicity of the Church: we must go forth as a Church and do the works of the Apostles. There is but one way of proving her Catholicity: we must bring her treasure to men of all races and nations, types and classes. There is but one way of proving her Sanctity: we must demonstrate her power to produce saints in the twentieth century.

And there is but one way to such faith—the way of prayer and intercession. Of late we have been much occupied with the respective merits of various forms and types of public worship, and our discovery that many of the old forms and types are outworn has made the whole subject of form and ritual assume a fictitious importance. Aids to prayer and facilities for devotional expression are poor substitutes for the apostolic spirit of prayer, and it is the spirit that is lacking. Only faith is needed, the faith that defies conventions, treads despondency under foot, is prepared to pray a whole lifetime without seeing any visible results, and works from beginning to end by love. Such faith is God's gift to all who dedicate themselves whole-heartedly to the apostolate of prayer.